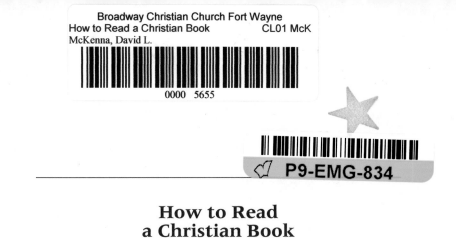

P9-EMG-834

How to Read
a Christian Book

Also by David L. McKenna

The Urban Crisis (1968)

Awake, My Conscience (1977)

The Jesus Model (1978)

The Communicator's Commentary: Mark (1982)

MegaTruth: The Church in the Age of Information (1986)

Power to Follow; Grace to Lead: Strategy for the Future of Christian Leadership (1986)

The Communicator's Commentary: Job (1986)

Renewing Our Ministry (1986)

The Whisper of His Grace (1987)

Discovering Job (1989)

Love Your Work (1989)

The Coming Great Awakening (1990)

The Works of Dr. David L. McKenna: Honoring Ten Years of Faithful Leadership at Asbury Theological Seminary (1992)

When Our Parents Need Us Most (1994)

The Communicator's Commentary: Isaiah 1–39 (1994)

The Communicator's Commentary: Isaiah 40–66 (1994)

A Future with a History: The Wesleyan Witness of the Free Methodist Church (1997)

Growing Up in Christ (1998)

Journey through a Bypass: The Story of an Open Heart (1998)

What a Time to Be a Wesleyan: Anticipating the Twenty-first Century (1999)

How to Read
a Christian Book

David L. McKenna

Baker Books
A Division of Baker Book House Co
Grand Rapids, Michigan 49516

© 2001 by David L. McKenna

Published by Baker Books
a division of Baker Book House Company
P.O. Box 6287, Grand Rapids, MI 49516-6287

Second printing, April 2001

Printed in the United States of America

Library of Congress Cataloging-in-Publication Data

McKenna, David L. (David Loren), 1929–
    How to read a Christian book / David L. McKenna.
        p.   cm.
    Includes bibliographical references.
    ISBN 0-8010-6359-0 (paper)
    1. Christians—Books and reading. 2. Christianity and literature.
    3. Best books. 4. Christian literature—History and criticism. I. Title.
    Z1039.C47M45   2001
    248.4'6—dc21   00-045439

For current information about all releases from Baker Book House, visit our web site:

http://www.bakerbooks.com

To
my sister,
Dr. Patricia McKenna Seraydarian,
an author of note whose writing career
has been temporarily disrupted by a stroke
but whose communication by faith, spirit, and wit continues
her ministry of encouragement to all who know her

Contents

Preface

Christians are reading more and more books. The sale of Christian books continues to be a boom industry—in bookstores, in supermarkets, and over the Internet. Certainly, nothing but good can come of our "print witness" amid the media of a secular society.

Yet, questions remain.

- We know the volume of sales of Christian books, but do we know the quality of their contents?
- We know which books are best-sellers in the Christian marketplace, but do we know whether Christians are reading with discernment?
- We know that millions of Christian books have been printed in the last fifty years, but do we know how many of them have the potential to become classics?
- We know that people are reading Christian books dealing with personal problems, but do we know whether Christians are understanding the faith and growing spiritually?

- We know that books of quality are being written by Christian scholars, but do we know whether books of substance are being produced for laypeople?
- We know that Christian books are being written to inspire, but do we know the value of Christian reading as a spiritual discipline?
- Most important of all, we know that millions of Christians are reading books, but do we know whether all the members of Christian homes, especially the younger generation, are among the readers?

Questions such as these provided the incentive for *How to Read a Christian Book.* The purpose of this book is simple and straightforward: As a lover of Christian books, I want to enhance the potential of their ministry by encouraging readers to choose books of quality, judge their content with discernment, develop a reading habit as a spiritual discipline, and build their own personal library. To accomplish these purposes, this book contains a three-year plan for reading contemporary books that meet the standards of biblical credibility, lay readability, literary quality, and developmental value to help Christians understand the Christian faith and grow spiritually. If these purposes are achieved, to God be the glory!

Acknowledgments

While one person may write a book, many people are part of the project. As author of *How to Read a Christian Book,* I owe a special word of thanks to those who shared the vision and supported the work. My thanks go to:

Dwight Baker, president of Baker Books

Donald Demaray, Senior Beeson Professor Emeritus of Homiletics at Asbury Theological Seminary

Sheila Lovell, executive assistant to the president at Asbury Theological Seminary

Janet McKenna, my wife of fifty years who loves to have me stay home and write in my retirement

Members of the selection committee who helped me choose the thirty-six books for the three-year reading plan.

Leith Anderson	Jack Hayford
Jill Briscoe	Jay Kesler
Maxie Dunnam	James Earl Massey
Ted Engstrom	Rebecca Manley Pippert
Vernon Grounds	Rick Warren

1. Why Christians Are Readers

In the beginning was the Word, and the Word was with God, and the Word was God.

John 1:1

R eading books comes naturally for Christians. Of course, the primer for all our reading is the Word of God. Together, we confess, "We are people of one Book." Yet, our reading is not limited to the Bible. We read book after book, which helps us understand and apply the Word of God. In the last half of the twentieth century, particularly, the publishing of Christian books became a major industry, offering readers thousands of titles at reasonable cost. Although we are reading more, we may not be reading what is best. More than likely, all believers would welcome assistance in selecting, reading, and collecting Christian books. First, however, we need to recall the roots of our reading. The progressive history of God's revelation not only reveals why Christians are natural readers, it also motivates us to read with the mind of the Spirit so that we may understand our faith and grow spiritually.

People of the Word

For Christians, the Word precedes the Book. In the first chapter of Genesis, we are introduced to the Word when God "spoke" the universe into existence, plants and animals into life, and human beings into his image. Behind the physical creation, however, is its spiritual essence. John, in his Gospel, takes us to the heart of the matter when he gives us the spiritual meaning of the creation story: "In the beginning was the Word" (John 1:1). Through the eyes of the Spirit, he sees that the Word is more than an uttered, impersonal phrase. The Word is God himself with all the attributes of his mind, spirit, and personality.

No human language is adequate to interpret the full meaning of "the Word" as revealed in John's Gospel. Synonymous with God himself, the Word is eternal and unfathomable. Even when we consider the Greek word *logos*, "the Word" defies easy definition. Because John was writing to people who understood Greek philosophy, he was inspired to use *logos* to define the deity of Jesus Christ and also explain the incarnation. Plato, foremost among Greek philosophers, divided all existence into spiritual ideals and physical realities.

He taught that an "ideal" exists in the eternal mind of the spiritual world and is imprinted in the physical world of material objects and human flesh. The ideal of "tree-ness," for instance, has been imprinted by some creative act into every species of trees. Consequently, even though there is infinite variety in trees, we still recognize them as trees because the ideal of "tree-ness" defines their nature and exists in our mortal minds.

To communicate with the Greek mind, John may have used the same analogy for the *logos*. To introduce Jesus Christ as very God of very God, he identified him as the ideal "Word" or *logos*. By opening his Gospel with the phrase "in the beginning was the Word," he drew a direct parallel with the opening of Genesis, "In the beginning, God." By connecting Plato's ideal in the eternal mind with Jesus Christ as the *logos,* John introduced his readers to the real and personal God of Christian faith. Taking the analogy one step further, he declared, "The Word was made flesh and dwelt among us" (John 1:14 KJV). This was a master stroke by which John confronted the Greeks with the claim of the incarnation. To Plato, when the ideal in the eternal mind was imprinted in "flesh," the ideal was contaminated. John says just the opposite. When the Word became flesh, the divine nature was unblemished in the glory of the one and only God and in the fullness of grace and truth as the Son of God. Greeks who understood Plato's ideal of "tree-ness" and its imprint in every species of tree, were challenged to see its application in the incarnation. In the life of Jesus Christ and in every word he spoke, they were asked to recognize the Word or *logos* as evidence of his divine and human nature. For us, as well, the challenge is apparent. We are people of the Word because we believe that all truth is God's truth and that Jesus Christ is the embodiment of that truth.

The Spoken Word

As the earliest expression of the Word, God spoke the world into being. The Genesis story of creation centers on God as a thinker (brooding over the chaos), a speaker (giving the order, "Let there be . . ."), a doer (choosing a task for each day of creation), and an appraiser (pronouncing his completed work "very good").

After his spoken act of creation, God continued to use direct and personal words to communicate with human beings. Whether with Adam in the Garden, Noah on the ark, Abraham on the plain, or Moses in the desert, God addressed his chosen leaders through intimate conversation, enjoying their fellowship and giving them detailed instructions for action. In these relationships, God asked that his people be listeners who pay close attention to his words, remember them carefully, and communicate them accurately to others. Sometimes we forget that God depended on his spoken Word for many generations. As fragile as that communication may seem, we know that the oral tradition of biblical revelation was God's truth as surely as any of his words that have been preserved in writing.

The Written Word

Communication between God and his human creation underwent a dramatic change when God himself became an author, writing the Ten Commandments on tablets of stone with his finger (Exod. 31:18). Moses had already started to write down all the detailed laws that God had dictated to him (Exod. 24:4), but the recording of the Ten Commandments opened a new era in which God spoke and humans wrote. At the point of transition between the oral and the written eras of the revelation of the Word, God instructed his people:

Hear, O Israel: The LORD our God, the LORD is one. Love the
LORD your God with all your heart and with all your soul and
with all your strength. These commandments that I give you
today are to be upon your hearts. Impress them on your children. Talk about them when you sit at home and when you
walk along the road, when you lie down and when you get
up. Tie them as symbols on your hands and bind them on
your foreheads. Write them on the doorframes of your houses
and on your gates.

Deuteronomy 6:4–9

The truth and beauty of these words echoed down through
biblical history. We notice that God summed up the complexity of the law in the simple truth, "Love the LORD your
God with all your heart and with all your soul and with all
your strength." Early on, God made it clear that the spirit of
the law superceded the letter of the law. Jesus confirmed that
truth when he quoted the same words in answer to the critic's
test question, "What is the greatest commandment?" Although human memory might fail to recall all the details of
the law, even the smallest child can learn and remember the
greatest commandment of all.

As the era advanced, the Word became more and more per-
manent in the writing of scribes and prophets throughout the
Old Testament. Even though the written Word was now an
indirect means of divine revelation, the truth of the message
was not compromised. God chose the written Word as the
means to preserve the truth for all generations and make it
available to all people. With that decision, he also expected
his people to be able, discerning, and obedient readers.

The Symbolic Word

God also gave Israel multimedia instructions for remembering his Word. Hebrew families were to teach the commandments to their children, talk about them in the activi-

ties of the day, represent them with symbols that could be worn on the body, and write them on the doorposts and gates of their homes. Israelites who followed God's instructions created a home school curriculum for teaching their children, made talk of God a natural part of their conversations, fashioned frontlets to hang over their foreheads as symbols reminding them of God's commandments, and etched God's Word on the doorposts of their homes. Behind these acts was God's singular purpose: He wants his people to remember his Word. In fact, the theme for the Book of Deuteronomy is "remember."

Throughout history, symbols have continued to remind Christians of truths found in the written Word. The cross, a lamb, a shepherd, bread, blood, and a dove are just a few examples. Because human beings are natural symbol-makers, our understanding of the faith is enhanced by these visual images. Without a doubt, God has used symbols to bring the Word to life.

The Living Word

With the coming of Jesus Christ, the most radical transformation of the Word took place. In his incarnation, he was "the Word" of whom John wrote in the introduction to his Gospel. All human history comes to its watershed in John's inspired perception: "The Word became flesh and made his dwelling among us. We have seen his glory, the glory of the One and Only, who came from the Father, full of grace and truth" (John 1:14).

No longer do we have to await the spoken Word of God in direct communication, wait until he writes on tablets of stone, interpret the symbolic Word on a doorpost, or depend on prophets for the written Word. In answer to our prayer, Jesus Christ became God with a face. As John wrote in his epistle, "That which was from the beginning, which we have heard, which we have seen with our eyes, which we have looked at and our hands have touched—this we proclaim concerning the Word of life" (1 John 1:1).

Nothing more needs to be said or read about the truth of God's Word. John's identification of Jesus Christ in the flesh as "the Word of life" affirmed Jesus' deity as the Son of God and his role as our Savior. Moreover, John attested to the finality of Jesus as the living Word. In Jesus and his words, all truth is revealed and all salvation is complete. As Jesus himself said, "Heaven and earth will pass away, but my words will never pass away" (Matt. 24:35). All other Christian words are commentary.

But we cannot stop here. By definition, the living Word is dynamic, not static. Just as John described Jesus as a living, breathing, changing, and growing human organism whom people could touch and feel, the Word of life continues to be fully alive among us through the presence of the Holy Spirit. If we believe anything less, we make Jesus Christ an artifact of history and his Word a static truth of limited contemporary value. Neither is true. For those who believe, the living presence of Jesus Christ and the relevance of his Word is as real today as when he walked and talked on earth. Eternal, final, alive, and relevant—these adjectives describe the living Word.

The Inspired Word

Just as Moses wrote down the laws spoken by God as a record for remembrance, other writers were instructed and inspired by his Spirit to write the full story of the living Word in books that now comprise the Old and New Testaments. Over the course of many years, these books were collected by church fathers and put to the test of whether or not their message was true to the revelation of Jesus Christ as the Son of God and Savior of the world. Like a thread running through every book from Genesis to Revelation, the story of the living Word unfolds. In Genesis, the coming of the Savior is prophesied when the Lord God speaks to the serpent and says, "He will crush your head and you will strike his heel" (Gen. 3:15). In Revelation, the return of the Savior is foreseen when John the Revelator concludes his vision with the benediction, "Amen. Come, Lord Jesus" (Rev. 22:20). In between, the Old Testament drama unfolds in anticipation of the Christ, comes to fulfillment in the Gospels, and unfolds again in the mission of the church to take the message of Christ to all nations.

Every book of the Old and New Testaments meets the test of contributing to the revelation of the living Word. To meet that test, their authors had to be inspired by the Spirit to write the text with the authority, accuracy, and consistency of God's truth. Although Christians may differ in their definitions of inspiration, they agree that the inspired Word of God in biblical writing is final truth and all-sufficient for our salvation. Paul, in his familiar words to Timothy, gives us a working definition of the Scriptures in which all believers find common ground: "All Scripture is God-breathed and is useful for teaching, rebuking, correcting and training in righteousness, so that the man of God may be thoroughly equipped for every good work" (2 Tim. 3:16–17).

The Dynamic Word

Christians need no other reason to be avid readers of the Word of God. Realizing that Scripture is "God-breathed" is motivation enough. Immediately, we see a connection between the living Word and the written Word. Just as Jesus Christ the living Word is an ever present and dynamic reality, the written Word is equally alive and active through the mind of the Holy Spirit. Every time we open the Scriptures, we should expect a personal encounter with the God-breathed Spirit of the living Word. This is reading at its very best. When the mind and spirit of a biblical author interact in vibrant dialogue with the mind and spirit of a reader, the highest purpose of the inspired Word is fulfilled. We should soar every time we read the Word of God.

The Teaching Word

In his letter to Timothy, Paul also addressed the learning process associated with the God-breathed Scriptures. The Scriptures were not written in esoteric language for philosophers or in religious language for theologians. Rather, Paul wrote that they are "useful for teaching, rebuking, correcting and training in righteousness." In the language of the teacher, the Scriptures offer a full curriculum for spiritual development. "Teaching" transmits God's truth, "rebuking" disciplines ungodly behavior, "correction" keeps us true to the Word, and "instruction in righteousness" rewards the Christlike life. Again, we should enthusiastically welcome the teaching-learning experience of the God-breathed Word, even when that experience includes rebuke and correction as well as teaching and training in righteousness. As with any sound educational experience, when we reflect on what we have learned in the Word of God, we are grateful for the disciplines of rebuke and correction as much as for the affirmations of teaching and training.

The Equipping Word

True to the principles of sound learning, Paul goes beyond the teaching-learning process to the goal of reading the God-breathed Word. We read, ". . . so that the man of God may be thoroughly equipped for every good work." A lofty goal, indeed, yet one that can be achieved in the life of every believer who is a diligent, lifelong student of the written Word. Through our encounters with the God-breathed Word and the Spirit-guided process of learning, we are equipped in every sphere of activity to do every good work. The claim is as lofty as the goal, yet each of us knows that when we are students of the living Word, we obtain the resources for daily living and Christian witness that qualify us as men and women of God. It is when we fail to immerse ourselves in the written witness of the living Word that we come up short on spiritual resources and fail in good works. Reading the written Word can never be a casual or optional exercise. If we are to be God's people "thoroughly equipped for every good work," we need to be eager students searching for truth, obeying his commands, and following his Spirit.

Taken together, then, Paul's words to Timothy give us the pattern for all our reading. First, we must connect with the dynamic spirit as well as the mind of the author. Second, we must submit ourselves to the teaching, rebuke, correction, and training of the text. Third, we must become persons better equipped for effective action in whatever realm we serve. As students of the Word of God, then, each of these aspects of our reading takes on supernatural and spiritual dimensions that are unique in regard to the Scriptures. Reading the Bible is not the same as reading other books. When we pick up other books to read, we ask the question, "Is it true?" If the answer is yes, we pay particular attention to that book. When we pick up the Bible, however, we do not ask that question. Because it is the God-breathed Word, we read it as the truth. Admittedly, millions of people read the Bible only as a piece of great literature, believing it possesses no more claim to truth than any other classic work. Still others approach the Bible with the eye of a critic, daring the text to stand the test of truth. Someplace in between are searching readers who would put the same sign over the Bible that a British person once proposed for the entrance to churches: "Important, if true."

Believers appreciate the literary quality of the Bible and have confidence that its message will stand the critic's test. But because we believe the Bible is true, we cannot just pass it off as "important." If it is true, we must obey it, and if it is true, it will change our lives.

Mortimer Adler and Charles Van Doren, in their celebrated book *How to Read a Book,* from which we draw time and again, include a section entitled "How to Read 'Canonical' Books." Using the Bible as an example, Adler and Van Doren say that this "sacred" writing or "holy" book must be read reverentially by believers who accept it as the truth and are thereby obliged to make sense out of it.[1] We would go a step farther. Not only must we accept the Bible as truth and make sense out of it, but we must enter into its spirit, obey its commands, and let it change our lives. For this reason, we understand why Adler and Van Doren also write, "There have been more books written about how to read Scripture than about all other aspects of the art of reading together. The Word of God is obviously the most difficult writing men can read, but it is also, if you believe it is the Word of God, the most important to read."[2] We agree. If we believe that the Bible is the Word of God, it is the most important reading we can do. More than that, it is reading that is essential to our salvation. Christians are people of one Book in which we find the truth that sets us free.

A word of caution is necessary here: Even though Christians are people of one Book, we are not guilty of what some critics call "Bibliolatry." We read the written Word, but we do not worship it. We do not believe that "the Word became ink and lives among us." We remember that long before the Scriptures were written, God communicated through the spoken Word. And long before the Scriptures were mass produced for all people to read, the text of the inspired manuscripts was preserved intact and communicated faithfully by our church fathers. Behind each of these means of communication is the living Word—coexistent with the Father and personalized in Jesus Christ. The inspired Word, therefore, is only a glimpse of the whole truth, which is the realm of God. While the Bible is totally true and all-sufficient for our salvation, we neither worship the written Word nor assume that after reading the text of the Bible we have nothing more to learn about the living Word. God has a whole new world of truth for us to discover.

Another word of caution is also necessary: Christians are people of one Book who do not need another revelation to know the truth. When our church fathers, under the guidance of the Holy Spirit, closed the canon of the Old and New Testaments, the revelation was final. Any other book that makes that claim is false; any sect that makes any other revelation, written or spoken, equal to the Bible is a cult. Furthermore, any religious movement that combines the Bible with any other claim to truth must be rejected by Christians. Because of the subtlety of many movements, Christians must be constantly alert to their influence. In such cases, two questions will usually expose falsehood: "Is Jesus Christ the living Word our one and only hope for salvation?" and "Is the written Word our final and infallible authority for truth?"

While the ability to discern truth and falsehood is essential to the thoroughly equipped man or woman of God, spiritual development through the God-breathed Word involves much more. With the goal of being equipped for "every good work," we need both character and competence. Character is the integrity of life in Christ that makes the work of Christians "good." Competence is the exercise of natural and spiritual gifts in the work that we do. Together with the teaching of the indwelling Holy Spirit, the Word of God brings us to our full potential as servants of the Lord Jesus Christ.

The Fulfilling Word

While the written Word is final, it is not static. Multiple references in Scripture remind us that God has more to say to us. John, in the last word of his Gospel, writes, "This is the disciple who testifies to these things and who wrote them down. We know that his testimony is true. Jesus did many other things as well. If every one of them were written down, I suppose that even the whole world would not have room for the books that would be written" (John 21:24–25).

Did John know how prophetic his words would be? Without a Christian bias, Adler and Van Doren conclude that more books have been written about Jesus Christ and his revelation than any other text in human history. The whole world hardly has room for the works that qualify as expositions on the fulfilling Word. We should not be surprised. When Jesus promised his disciples the coming of the Holy Spirit, he said, "I have much more to say to you, more than you can now bear" (John 16:12). As a model for all teachers, Jesus knew the learning limits of his disciples. Intellectually, emotionally, and spiritually, Jesus' announcement that he would leave them pushed the limits of their understanding. After his death, resurrection, and ascension, they would need time to absorb this truth before he could teach them its implications for the salvation of the world and their part in the redemptive plan.

A good teacher also knows how to balance uncomfortable truth with words of encouragement. Jesus gave his disciples encouraging words when he immediately followed his shocking news with the affirmative announcement, "But when he, the Spirit of truth, comes, he will guide you into all truth" (John 16:13). Here is the first call to lifelong learning. With the Holy Spirit as their teacher and "all truth" as the sphere of learning, the disciples were assured that their teaching-learning experience would be continued with the same personal attention and powerful impact that they had known at the feet of Jesus.

Following the Gospels, the rest of the New Testament continues the story of the fulfilling Word. Fulfillment begins with Peter's sermon at Pentecost, when he interpreted Christ's death and resurrection with uncanny perception, and continues through to John's prophetic revelation on the island of Patmos. Truth in both word and deed is fulfilled in the New

Testament story as the Holy Spirit applies the living Word to the work of the Great Commission. When Jesus said to his disciples, "Greater works than these shall you do," he gave them the promise of the fulfilling Word.

The teaching of the Holy Spirit did not end with the final sentence of the Book of Revelation. Christian history is replete with evidence of the fulfilling Word. Even today, as we read the Word of God, the Holy Spirit guides us into all truth. No other book is as universal and timeless as the Bible. Its truth is as fresh today as it was when it was written. In one way or another, every circumstance of life is addressed. We can affirm with confidence the truth that the fulfilling Word is the all-sufficient guide for our conduct as well as the only way to our salvation.

The Word and Truth

Our Source of Truth

Implicit in the promise that the Spirit will guide us into all truth are two premises underlying all human words and writing. First, all truth is God's truth. However deep or far the human mind may move in the search for truth, nothing is outside the realm of God. Every book that has ever been written is within the scope of God's truth. Second, all truth is centered in Jesus Christ. As a circle must have a center, the whole realm of truth must have a point of reference. When Paul described the supremacy of Jesus Christ, he wrote, "He is before all things, and in him all things hold together" (Col. 1:17). Whether or not authors throughout the centuries acknowledged the living Word on which all other words depend, the fact remains that all human knowledge turns on the centrality of Jesus Christ. Secular or sacred, all books will be judged by the question, "Is it true to the Word of God as revealed in Jesus Christ?"

Jesus' promise to his disciples is also our legacy. We too are called to be lifelong learners of unfolding truth taught to us by the Holy Spirit. The promise applies, first, to the Word of God. Only as the Holy Spirit teaches us can we grasp the meaning of the truth for our personal needs and social responsibilities. Second, it applies to the sermons we hear, the teaching we experience, and the books we read. Beware of believers who say they need no help interpreting the Word of God and understanding the mind of Christ as it applies to us today. Without the presence of the Holy Spirit as our teacher, we are vulnerable to dangerous and sometimes demonic applications of the Word of God. Extremist pro-lifers, for instance, who bomb abortion clinics and murder abortion doctors distort the Word to justify evil. Only with the mind of the Holy Spirit can we become learning Christians who discern the truth and show the love of Jesus Christ.

The Body of Christ—Our Friends in Truth

We need others to join with the Holy Spirit as our teachers. In a familiar story in the Book of Acts, an Egyptian eunuch was returning home from Jerusalem and reading the prophecy of Isaiah as he rode along in his chariot. Philip, following the instructions of the Holy Spirit, ran up to the chariot and asked, "Do you understand what you are reading?" The eunuch answered, "How can I unless someone explains it to me?" Philip then joined him on the ride and explained how the prophet Isaiah was forecasting the good news about Jesus Christ. Needing no more evidence, the eunuch believed and was baptized (Acts 8:26–40).

Christian Books—Our Tools for Truth

For us as well, God provides many sources to help us understand the Word of God with the Holy Spirit as our teacher.

Christian books are one of those sources. Although they should never be substituted for the Word of God itself, they can be invaluable teaching aids that the Holy Spirit can use to illuminate the truth and apply it to our lives. Just as Philip climbed up in the eunuch's chariot to explain the Scriptures to him, Christian books can meet us where we are in our daily lives and reveal the meaning of the Scriptures. This assumes, of course, that we are, first of all, readers of the Word of God and students of the Holy Spirit. If so, Christian books, like guideposts along the way of our spiritual journey, can help keep us on course and point the way to our destination.

The Case for Reading Christian Books

Returning to our opening question, "Why are Christians natural readers of books?" a summary of the above discussion provides the answer:

- God is the Word, the source of all truth.
- God has progressively revealed himself to us through the spoken Word and the written Word.
- Jesus Christ, the living Word of God, is the source and center of all truth—eternal and unchanging.
- The Bible is inspired by God as the written Word of truth—final and infallible.
- The meaning and application of the living Word continues to be revealed to us through the teaching of the Holy Spirit.
- All other words, spoken or written, are commentary on the living Word that help us understand our faith and grow spiritually.

- Christian books, read with a discerning mind open to the teaching of the Holy Spirit, are key sources for helping us understand our faith and grow spiritually.

An adventure awaits us in reading Christian books. Once we see the connection between the Word of God and the books we read, we will embark on a search and discovery mission in the expanding field of human knowledge, where all truth is God's truth and Jesus Christ is the center that holds all things together. A nonreading Christian is a contradiction in terms. With the Bible as our primary source, we read other books that serve as teaching tools for the Holy Spirit in order that we may become men and women of God, "thoroughly equipped for every good work."

❖

2. Choosing a Christian Book

How much better to get wisdom than gold,
to choose understanding rather than silver!

Proverbs 16:16

Millions of Christian books have been written since the time of Christ, and tens of thousands have been published in the last fifty years. Some are classics that have stood the test of time, some are best-sellers that enjoyed a season of popularity, some are throwaways that should never have been printed, and many others are located somewhere in between. Because we cannot read every book in order to judge its quality for ourselves, we need to ask the question, "How can I select Christian books of quality that will help me understand the faith and grow spiritually?"

As we think about this question, we realize that we often select Christian books in a rather haphazard manner. Most often, we hear about a book by word-of-mouth from a friend who is reading the book. Or if we are part of a small group ministry, we may become aware of a book after it's selected by the leader or the group for reading and study. Again, our pastor might refer to a book in a sermon, which prompts us to buy and read it. Occasionally, we might see ads or reviews in Christian magazines for books written by well-known authors whose works have been particularly helpful to us. Bestsellers, of course, come to our attention through the announcements of annual book awards. Managers of Christian bookstores may point us to a book that addresses a personal need we may have at a given point in time.

By and large, then, we tend to select Christian books in highly personal and random ways. Each of the methods we have identified is good, but can we do better? Each of us knows the frustration of buying a book from which we learn little and find few answers to the questions we may have. Without taking the fun out of searching for books, a more systematic approach can help us find quality books that address our needs. Here are some steps toward that goal.

Be a Listener

Many good books come to our attention when we listen to other readers who recommend books and authors to us. I reserve the flyleaf of my date book for the titles of books that others suggest. Five titles are currently on the page awaiting my next trip to the Christian bookstore. Better yet, ask your friends, "What book are you reading right now? What is your opinion about the book? Would you recommend that I read it?"

During my years as a college, university, and seminary president, I developed a special set of questions for job interviews with prospective faculty and administrators. After working through the standard questions about professional qualifications and personal commitments, I would surprise the candidate by asking, "What book, other than the Bible, are you reading or have recently read that you would recommend to me?" Oftentimes, I learned more about the person from this inquiry than from all the standard questions combined. Before long, I began to make the observation: We are what we read. Some candidates went blank when I asked them the question. Others grasped for straws and came up with a title of a popular book of light fiction or a Christian book of relational fluff. But for others, the question lighted a dancing fire in their eyes. Animation and passion took over as they described a book, spun out its theme, and recommended it for my reading. Before long, I began to ask the question earlier in my interviews because I saw a connection between the act of reading and the growth potential of the reader. Whether in a formal job interview or a personal chat, if we ask a similar question and then listen for the answer, more often than not it will open the way for a good conversation and provide a source for selecting good books.

Be a Looker

Like the advice given to a kindergartener before he crosses a street, we need to stop, look, and listen before we select a Christian book. Another bit of advice that I have found helpful in choosing books to read is to look around the homes we visit to see what the residents are reading. The first look is to the coffee table. Interior decorators tell us that the items on a coffee table reveal the personality of the family. With this thought in mind, in our home my wife and I have open Bibles on our coffee tables in the living and family rooms so that all visitors will know that the Word of God shapes the personality of our home. Remembering that children become readers by picking up books around the house and seeing their parents reading, we also keep Christian books we are reading next to the Bible on the coffee table.

This insight stood me in good stead when I served as a Christian college and university president. My travels took me across the country into the homes of alumni, students, and prospective students. A look at the coffee tables in those homes spoke volumes to me. I would also cast glances at the magazine rack and the bookshelves. With uncanny accuracy, I could predict whether or not our alumni were lifelong readers and whether or not our prospective students came from homes where good books and periodicals were read. Frankly, the results were disappointing. I concluded that advanced reading for most homes included the Bible, *Time* magazine, and a popular Christian book on interpersonal relationships.

Be a looker. Begin in your own home and ask what signals you want to send to your family, friends, and strangers. In the field of reading development, experts tell us that the presence of books in the home and evidence that parents read are the greatest incentives for young readers. Certainly, the same advice applies to Christians who want their children to be readers of the Word and other worthwhile books.

Be a looker in other homes as well. Especially when you visit Christian friends in whom you see spiritual growth, look for books they have chosen for their own reading. Pulling those books off the shelf and asking your friend for a recommendation will usually spark a lively conversation. Just recently, I visited the home of a Christian colleague and noticed *The Ragamuffin Gospel* on the table. Intrigued by the title,

I picked up the book and asked my host about it. He was surprised that I hadn't heard about the ministry of the author, Brennan Manning, who taught my friend the meaning of unconditional love. I wrote down the title and name of the author in my daybook and ordered the book as soon as I could. Christian friends who read with discernment and show evidence of their reading in their spiritual growth are an invaluable resource for choosing Christian books.

Be a Surfer

Within the past year or so, a whole new world of books has opened up to us through the Internet. Anyone who is online with a personal computer has access to sources that provide information on millions of books. The mind can become dizzy when confronted with the speed at which an author, a book, or a subject is flashed on the screen, but at the same time, where else can we gain immediate access to a synopsis of the text, reviews by critics, letters from readers, and instructions for ordering the book at a discount. While for many, these Internet sources cannot replace the quiet and reflective hours that true lovers of books experience in libraries and bookstores, they do offer speed of delivery at a competitive price. Their greatest value, however, is that they provide an opportunity to read reviews from readers, learn about other books related to the subject, and enter into online conversations with others who have read the book.

Be a Browser

Although futurists in the field of technology may argue that the text is dead, they fail to understand the incomparable joys of browsing in bookstores. I have often said that a visit to a bookstore "cleanses my soul." Alone in the presence of great minds and new ideas, I experience a communion of mind and spirit that the best of electronic screens cannot duplicate. Of course, the new technology with its E-books does have advantages, such as instant retrieval of diverse sources and cross-referencing of complex subject matter, with which a single book can never compete. For book lovers, however, one disadvantage may well be the fact that you can't take an E-book into the bathtub with you. Many of us have the good memory of soaking in a book while soaking in a tub. Perhaps our reading habits will radically change in the next few years, but for some of us, the loss of leisure will be greater than the gain in efficiency.

Perhaps the greatest disadvantage associated with E-books is that you don't get to browse for them—at least not in a bookstore. Browsing in a bookstore is an art. Without a specific goal in mind, you begin by cruising the aisles to get an overview of the scene. If the bookstore manager is creative in marketing, the "hot" titles and authors jump out at you. Then, the table of bargain books catches your eye. Another move takes you along the shelves that hold books displayed alphabetically by author. Everyone has favorite authors, and it is natural to take a peek at the latest work he or she has written. Finally, you move to the specialty racks where the volumes are displayed according to subject matter. Usually, you give the most attention to the areas of your special interest. The approach to browsing in a bookstore is like taking a guided tour in a strange city to get the lay of the land. After seeing the scene in overview, you can return to the areas that pique your interest and warrant further investigation.

Browsing is also a science. Begin with titles. Although there are exceptions, most good books have good titles. This was not always true. Some of the greatest classics in the world are encumbered with stodgy titles. A *New Yorker* magazine published a cartoon in which Moses was chiseling the book of the law in tablets of stone. As an onlooker peered over Moses' shoulder, he said, "The text is good, but couldn't you think of a punchier title than Deuteronomy?" The same might be said of such earthshaking works as Martin Luther's *Preface to the Epistle to the Romans,* John Calvin's *Institutes of Christian Religion,* or John Wesley's *Journal.*

Today, however, titles of books must be marketable. Much time and attention is given to titles that not only reveal the subject of the book but also catch a reader's eye. Think, for instance, of C. S. Lewis's *Mere Christianity,* Oswald Chambers's *My Utmost for His Highest,* Richard Foster's *Celebration of Discipline,* Dietrich Bonhoeffer's *The Cost of Discipleship,* Elton Trueblood's *The Incendiary Fellowship,* John Perkins's *Let Justice Roll Down,* or Philip Yancey's *Where Is God When It Hurts?* Even if we didn't know the books or the authors, each of these titles would stop us in our tracks and invite us to open the book.

But be careful. Titles can also be deceptive. Sometimes they are like Forrest Gump's box of chocolates: "You never know what you're going to get." I recall, for instance, the title of a book prominently displayed in a bookstore that stopped me in my tracks. The book jacket read, "Lions 3; Christians 0." *Ah, ha,* I thought. *Here is a creative approach to the question of spiritual conflict.* Upon opening the book, however, I found that it was a fictional parody hardly matching the title. On the other hand, we should not write off books strictly on the basis of their titles. Eugene Peterson wrote a book entitled *A Long Obedience in the Same Direction.* In current market terms, the title may be too long to catch a reader's eye and stick in the memory. But it is consistent with the text of the book, and once you have read it, the spiritual impact will never be forgotten.

I have learned about good titles the hard way. A few years ago, I wrote a book on Christian leadership using the incarnation of Jesus as my model. When I submitted the manuscript, I suggested the title *Incarnational Leadership.* The editors felt the word *incarnational* was too theological to attract a wide readership, so they asked me to think again. After days of testing options, I finally suggested *Power to Follow; Grace to Lead* because it expressed the fact that the incarnation turned the secular model of leadership upside down. The editors loved the title and published the book. Since then, I have seldom met anyone who can correctly give the title when they mention the book. Invariably, they call it *Power to Lead; Grace to Follow.* Evidently, power is so aligned with leading and grace with following that our minds have difficulty making the opposite connection. Since then, I have become a student of titles in bookstores. Even now, as I look at the bookshelf above me, I see *Hard Drive,* the Bill Gates story by James Wallace and Jim Erickson, *Knowing God* by J. I. Packer, *Leadership without Power* by Max De Pree, *When Giants Learn to Dance* by Rosabeth Moss Kanter, *Undaunted Courage,* the story of Lewis and Clark by Stephen Ambrose, and *What's So Amazing about Grace?* by Philip Yancey. In each case, creativity in the title matches quality in the text. Although a creative title cannot guarantee a qualitative text, the art of browsing begins with a search for titles that pique our imagination and urge us to read the book.

Be a Sampler

An old adage says, "You can't tell a book by its cover." This is only partially true when selecting books to read. Modern books often have book jackets or back covers that provide a wealth of information. Without even opening a book, we should be able to make some judgments about its theme, author, and endorsements. A selective reader will sample the information available on the back cover and the flyleaf of a potential book.

Information about the author usually catches the eye first. Experienced readers of books often say, "If you don't know the author, make sure you know the publisher." There is wisdom in these words. Names of well-known or favorite authors are the best recommendations for the books we choose. You know what to expect and have some assurance of quality. There is no guarantee, however, that the quality of writing will continue from one book to another. Many literary critics argue that many authors have only one book in them. As with box office hits in the movie industry, sequels to bestselling books are often bombs. Still, we can usually count on good writers to keep writing good books.

If you don't know the author, a brief biography can be found on the back of the book, on its jacket, or at the end of the book. You can quickly learn something about the author's professional role, personal life, religious affiliation, and other writings. Usually, you can find enough information to help you determine whether you want to read farther.

The back cover or jacket also contains an excerpt or summary of the book, from which you can grasp the essence of the author's thoughts. Take, for example, Robert Wuthnow's book *Christianity in the Twenty-first Century: Reflections on the Challenges Ahead,* which is located on my bookshelf. The title itself tells us that this is a serious book probably of a scholarly nature. On the back cover, I read these words:

> In the year 2000—and beyond—what will the church be like? What challenges will it face? Will the church be able to provide a strong sense of community? Will it be an ethical force in the lives of Americans? And what role will religion play in politics and the marketplace?

At the bottom of the page, then, I read that the author is Robert Wuthnow, Gerhard R. Andlinger Professor of Social Sciences and Director of the Center for the Study of American Religion at Princeton University. Combining the sweeping questions with the scholarly credentials of the author, we know that the book would be a challenge for the average reader. This should not turn us off because the book jacket also promises that Wuthnow will demonstrate that "people of faith have strong reasons to enter the next century with confidence in their religious institutions." While there is no doubt that the book would be challenging to read, we also know it contains information pertinent to our lives as Christians facing a new century.

Let's contrast this with the back cover of a book I wrote called *Growing Up in Christ*. Rather than writing the blurb summarizing the book myself, I entrusted the task to the editors as a test of the clarity of my message. Readers who pick up the book and turn it over will find these words:

> When we feel the pangs of spiritual hunger, we sense the Spirit nudging us toward the holiness of God. It is in these growing places of the soul that we can learn the truth which Jesus taught—
>
> • Height Is Depth
> • Living Is Dying
> • More Is Less
> • Keeping Is Giving
>
> *Growing Up in Christ* will encourage individuals and study groups to reach for spiritual maturity.

After reading these words, anyone can decide whether or not to open the book. The theme is identified, the outline is given, and the market of potential readers is identified. Hopefully, curiosity is also piqued so that a potential reader will want to sample the text.

Book jackets and back covers also include endorsements from prominent persons. Little information can be gained from the words of the endorsements because they are solicited from persons who are willing to give a glowing commendation for the book. The names of those who endorse the book are more important. Because Billy Graham is so se-

*Choosing
a Christian
Book*

❖

37

lective with endorsements, his commendation of a book or author is tantamount to a best-seller. Others of note include Charles Colson, Mark Hatfield, Jill Briscoe, and Lloyd Ogilvie. Their endorsement of a book prompts us to ask, "If the text was meaningful for them, shouldn't I also read it?"

Ironically, it took more time to write these words than it would for you to get a bird's-eye view of a book that is yet to be opened. A quick scan lasting two or three minutes will give you much information you need to make a decision: Do I or do I not want to find out what is inside the covers?

Be a Prober

I must confess that I become acquainted with many books that I never buy. This is not cheating. Bookstore managers welcome probers as well as samplers. To probe a book that intrigues me, I open to the table of contents. Here again, the author's creativity comes through in the titles of the chapters. More important, however, the table of contents should reveal the author's theme in outline form. By reading chapter titles, you should get a sense of the movement of the book as the author addresses the theme. Going to my bookshelf again, I see J. I. Packer's book *Knowing God*. Three major divisions are located in the table of contents:

I. Know the Lord
II. Behold Your God!
III. If God Be for Us . . .

With clarity and creativity, one of our generation's brightest scholars and beloved teachers has invited us to read his book.

Still, the probing mind takes nothing for granted. Beginning with the table of contents, I pick out a chapter that particularly interests me. In this case, my eyes are drawn to chapter 20 entitled "Thou Our Guide." Turning to the indicated page for that chapter, I check out the first sentence. Long ago I learned that the opening words of a book or chapter set the tone for the entire text. In fact, I became a collector of opening sentences after reading that Charles Dickens's first line in *A Tale of Two Cities* is considered one of the greatest opening sentences in all literature. "It was the best of times; it was the worst of times" instantly grabs our attention, sticks in our memory, and creates anticipation for reading the book. Another classic opener comes with Ernest Hemingway's *Old Man and the Sea.* He begins with these words: "There was an old man who fished alone in a skiff in the Gulf Stream and he had gone eighty four days now without taking a fish." My favorite, however, is the opening line from Leo Tolstoy's *Anna Karenina:* "All happy families are like one another; each unhappy family is unhappy in its own way." My collection contains many other opening sentences, but ultimately none can compete with the Word of God itself. "In the beginning God created the heavens and the earth" stands alone as the most powerful and pungent truth ever spoken.

How does Packer's opening for the chapter "Thou Our Guide" stack up with the quality of other opening sentences? He begins, "To many Christians, guidance is a chronic problem." My first response is to ask, "How did he know that spiritual guidance is one of my problems?" In the mirror of his words, I see my need, but I also see the promise of help. Packer has grabbed my interest, and I am ready to read more. A scan of the subheadings in the chapter adds to that interest. They are:

God Has a Plan
How We Receive Guidance
Six Common Pitfalls
No Simple Answers
When We Miss the Road

Without reading any of the text, I know that the book has value for me. Oftentimes, I will also check the final page of the chapter to see if the author has written a summary. Many authors have different ways of summing up their thoughts. Packer chooses a summary sentence followed by a verse from a Wesley hymn and then a final quotation from Joseph Hart to seal his case for knowing God:

> 'Tis Jesus, the first and the last,
> Whose Spirit shall guide us safe home;
> We'll praise him for all that's past,
> And trust him for all that's to come.

In fisherman's language, I've got a "keeper." It's time to take the next step in choosing a Christian book.

Be a Buyer

When you find a book that is a keeper, it is time to buy. Not that you need to feel guilty about browsing through a bookstore, knowing that the manager needs to show a profit. Many times you will walk out of a bookstore without buying because none of the books you sampled met your standards for purchase. But when you find a book that meets the standards, you should buy it for three good reasons.

First of all, you should buy a book in order to make it your own. Begin to think of reading a book as an ongoing conversation between you and the author. You will want to feel free to use a highlighter to note key thoughts, and you will want to write your own thoughts in the margins. To a certain extent, a clean book is an unread book. Even though you may understand the message of the author and remember some key thoughts, you are still a passive reader at the receiving end of one-way communication. Moments ago, I returned to a book that I had read as a source for a speech. Fluorescent yellow highlights set off key sentences of the text. Circled numbers over sequential thoughts and marginal notes fill the book. Within minutes I was able to revisit the entire book, find the quotes I needed, and gain some new insights on the way. In a very personal way, the book belongs to me.

Second, you should buy a book in order to build your own library. A personal library is a prized possession. Its books represent your signature in reading. Take a look at the books on your reading shelf. What do they say about you? Do you read widely in both Christian and secular literature? Do you read deeply in one subject or another? Do you have both classics and contemporary books in your collection? Who is your favorite author?

I see a personal library as a "poor person's art collection." At the most reasonable cost, a gallery of great works can be collected, displayed, and immediately accessible to its owner. Moreover, that gallery can be shared with others. When I retired and decided to give away almost three thousand books from my personal library, I had the thrill of giving them to a new evangelical seminary in Eastern Europe. One of my former students followed up the gift by visiting the seminary and building the bookshelves for the collection. He took pictures of the project and sent them to me. Most important, however, the number of books I gave allowed the seminary to gain recognition from the state so it could function as an educational institution.

Third, we need to buy books so that we have ready access to key sources when we or others are dealing with personal issues or when we are preparing to teach or speak. Individual books from my library are scattered across the world and are in the hands of students and friends to whom I lent them. When I chat or counsel with people, I have a tendency to ask, "Have you read this book?" Most often, they say, "No," and I promise to send them a copy from my library. Just recently, for instance, I was involved in a conversation with a Christian couple who felt they had been severely wronged by a brother. On two occasions, I listened as they went deep into a well of bitterness and came up saying that they were trying to forgive, but they couldn't forget. Their words prompted me to ask, "Have you read Lewis Smedes's book *Forgive and Forget?*" When they answered, "No," I promised them my copy and took it to them personally. Now, I have to replace the book in my library because it is one of those volumes to which I turn again and again.

Even though we may not be preachers, most Christians are offered, at one time or another, the opportunity to teach or speak about the faith. When those moments come, we need resources in addition to the Word from which to draw. Our personal library is the starting point. Whether it is a reference source, such as a biblical concordance through which we can trace key words, or a classical work, such as St. Augustine's *Confessions,* or a contemporary volume, such as C. S. Lewis's *Mere Christianity,* having ready access to quality Christian books is helpful. A church or local library and searches over the Internet will give us an expanded base for locating books, but there is no substitute for having a core collection within arm's reach on our own library shelves.

A rich experience awaits us as we enter the ever widening world of Christian books. We can think of ourselves as adventurers in the quest for hidden treasures. Our search for books will have its own intrigue, our selection of books will be most rewarding, and our collection of books will be like jewels of great price. Intellectually and spiritually, then, we will become partners with the apostle Paul, who wrote to Timothy from his prison cell in Rome, "When you come, pick up Mark and bring him with you. . . . And please bring with you the cloak I left with Carpus at Troas, and the books, especially the manuscripts" (2 Tim. 4:11, 13 PHILLIPS). As Paul needed Mark to keep him spiritually encouraged and his cloak to keep him physically warm, he needed his books and his writing to keep him intellectually alive. Our needs are no different. Along with the Word of God, Christian books are like good friends and warm clothes. We need them all.

3. Judging a Christian Book

And this is my prayer: that your love may abound more and
more in knowledge and depth of insight, so that you may be
able to discern what is best.

Philippians 1:9–10

In one sense, we judge Christian books as we do any other
book. We expect them to meet the standards of good writing. The purpose of the book should be clear and its outline
concise. Furthermore, we expect the author to be honest in

the presentation of facts, cogent in argument, and convincing in conclusion, whether we agree or not. When we finish a book, we should be able to answer these questions:

What is the book about?
What issues does it address?
What questions does it raise?
What difference does it make in my life?
What should I as a Christian do with the information it contains?

A Christian book that does not meet standards of literary quality and does not answer these questions is not worthy of our time and attention. That's why skimming a book and giving it a superficial reading are valuable exercises for deciding whether a book is worth reading more slowly and in depth.

While quality writing is important when judging a book, Christian books should meet an even higher standard. As mentioned earlier, because the canon of Scripture is the final authority for the revelation of God's truth, all other Christian writing is commentary. This means that all Christian writing should be judged against the standard of the Word of God. For this reason, Christian books are a breed of their own in the literary world and are subject to a more rigorous test of truth than books that claim no connection to the Word. Of course, in the long term, all human writing will be judged true or false in relationship to God's revelation. For now, however, the standard applies most directly to distinctly Christian writing.

The Biblical Standard of Scripture

No one can dispute the standard that the Word of God sets for itself. The expectations are high and clear. Under the inspiration of the Holy Spirit, Paul wrote to Timothy: "Every

Scripture is inspired by God and is useful for teaching, for reproof, for correction, and for instruction in right doing; so that the man of God may be complete, perfectly equipped for every good work" (2 Tim. 3:16–17 Weymouth).

This landmark sentence of biblical revelation addresses three questions:

1. What is the *nature* of Scripture?
   "Every Scripture is inspired by God."
2. What is the *function* of Scripture?
   "Every Scripture is . . . useful for teaching, for reproof, for correction, and for instruction in right doing."
3. What is the *goal* of Scripture?
   ". . . that the man of God may be complete, perfectly equipped for every good work."

Lofty claims indeed. But claims that set the Word of God apart from all other writing. Christian believers do not approach the Word with the skeptical question, "Is it true?" Rather, with faith and trust, we accept God's claim at face value and declare it "the whole truth and nothing but the truth."

Such a statement of faith is not without its complications. If the Scriptures are true, we must then ask, "What do I do about the truth?" Again, the answer is clear. When we read the Scriptures, we open ourselves to the tools of truth that the Holy Spirit uses as our teacher. First, there is the "teaching" of the truth of biblical doctrine. Second, there is the "reproof" of falsehood. Third, we encounter the "correction" of truth that brings us back to the path of righteousness when we stray. Fourth, the "instruction" of truth points us toward righteous living.

Note that teaching and reproof deal with doctrine whereas correction and instruction deal with behavior. Also, note that teaching and instruction are in a sense affirmative teaching tools while reproof and correction are disciplines. As any good teacher knows, students need to be taught content and conduct as well as disciplined by affirmation and negation in order to achieve the goal of learning. Paul identifies the goal of all Christian education when he writes, ". . . that the man [or woman] of God may be complete, perfectly equipped for every good work."

God has to be either a starry-eyed idealist about our potential for spiritual development or a down-to-earth realist with full confidence in the teaching ability of the Holy Spirit to make this claim. So many of us fall far short of spiritual maturity defined in these terms. We are reluctant to claim that we are men and women of God, complete and "perfectly equipped for every good work." Yet, as educators know, students respond best to expectations that are high, clear, and consistent. Therefore, even though most of us do not reach the ideal of spiritual maturity as defined by Scripture, we are motivated to strive toward the ideal. Better yet, we realize that God has established a lifelong learning process for us. Paul had that confidence when he wrote, ". . . being confident of this, that he who began a good work in you will carry it on to completion until the day of Jesus Christ" (Phil. 1:6). Each of us can claim that promise as we read the Word and invite the Holy Spirit to be our teacher. To our surprise, we will find that we are growing more godly, becoming better equipped to live the Christian life, and doing more good works than we ever imagined.

Paul's words to Timothy also serve as a check and balance on our spiritual development. Unless we read the Word of God, we cannot be instructed by the Spirit, and unless we are instructed by the Spirit, we cannot become godly and effective servants. To put it another way, loving the Word, learning from the Word, and living out the Word are interlocked in God's plan for our spiritual growth. A lapse in one can cause a lapse in another. Conversely, a gain in one will create a gain in another. By self-examination on each of these points, we can readily assess our spiritual development.

Relating Christian Books to the Word of God

What then is the relationship between the Word of God and other Christian books? At one and the same time, the realms of reading are both independent and interdependent. As the God-breathed Word, Scripture stands alone as God's revelation. No other Christian book can make this claim. None of them can stand alone without the Scriptures. But any of them can serve to increase our understanding of the truth, enrich the teaching-learning process of the Holy Spirit, and speed our development as mature and effective servants of the Lord Jesus Christ. Christian books, then, must be judged by the standards of Scripture rewritten to apply to commentary on the Word itself. These standards can be framed as questions that we should ask of every Christian book.

Is This Book True to the Inspired Word of God?

We can readily sort out distinctly Christian books from mere religious books when faced with this question. For a period of ten years, I served as the editor for a periodical called the *Minister's Personal Library.* Each month I received a box of the latest books that I had to consider recommending to ministers. Sometimes the author, the title, or the publisher became a dead giveaway that a book was religious but not Christian. At one extreme, I received a copy of a book written by a radical feminist who rewrote the creation story with vivid sex symbols in order to justify lesbian love. On the other extreme, I examined a book written by an ultra-fundamentalist who relied heavily on Scripture to stake the claim that he and he alone had a corner on God's truth.

Books at these extremes sorted themselves out. Other books were less obvious in their position. Evangelicals, for instance, went through a period when they were very interested in books on counseling and psychology. I put these books to the same test question: "Is this book true to the inspired Word of God?" Many of the books failed the test even though their authors were evangelical Christians who would ascribe to the full inspiration and final authority of Scripture. In their writing, however, they used the Scriptures to sanctify their psychology. In some cases, therapy and theology clashed without the author knowing the difference. The Word of God will not take second place to any human theory. It cannot be used as a proof text to justify a position or distorted to fit a case we want to present. Scripture is like God himself: It will be all or it will be not at all.

From my experience as an editor, then, I realized that the first test question included two other questions. One, "Is this book true to the *text* of the Word?" In other words, does the author accept the accuracy of the inspired Scriptures? A second question followed naturally: "Is this book true to the *spirit* of the Word?" Although the Word speaks with a surgical cut on such issues as sin, its overriding spirit is the hope of redemption.

Each of us has had the experience of reading a Christian book whose story marched across the pages like a parade of wooden soldiers. In the language of students, "The book was as dry as dust." Works of systematic theology or church history are usually put in this category without a fair reading. Thomas Oden's books on Christology, however, prove that theology can be true to the text and true to the spirit of the Word at one and the same time. As we read Oden, we sense that we are reading theology cast as a love story. The author would be the last to claim that his writing was inspired, but no one can doubt that he had the mind of the Spirit in both text and tone as he wrote. In a very real sense, Oden captured the dynamic of the God-breathed Word as he wrote his commentary on Christ.

Is This Book Useful for Christian Teaching?

After identifying the nature of the Word as inspired by God, Paul makes it clear that the Scriptures are not an esoteric text without practical application. On the contrary, he says that the Scriptures are "useful" tools for teaching, reproof, correction, and instruction in right doing. Never let it be said that the Word of God does not apply to our daily life. If its claims are true, the Scriptures give us everything that is necessary, not just for our salvation but for living in the contemporary world as well.

Earlier, we noted that teaching and instruction are affirmative teaching tools, while reproof and correction are disciplines. We also noted that both are essential for effectiveness in the teaching-learning process. As any of us must admit, we have learned as much from reproof and correction as we have from teaching and instruction.

Now, however, we need to look at these teaching tools of Scripture in a different way. We see a distinction not just between affirmative tools and discipline but between the teaching of *what to believe* and *how to behave*. Teaching refers specifically to true doctrine, while reproof addresses issues of false doctrine. Correction, then, deals with questions of wrong behavior, and instruction in right doing points toward right behavior.

Each of us can recall moments when the study of Scripture helped us understand true doctrine of the Christian faith. We may also remember times when the Word rebuked false doctrine that might otherwise have contaminated what we believe. An example comes to mind. When I spoke at the World Methodist Council in Nairobi, Africa, in 1987, I chose a biblical text consistent with the theme "Jesus Christ, the Only Hope for Our Salvation." The Gospel of John records the story of Jesus preaching the truth about himself and his mission to the masses, religious leaders, his followers, and the Twelve. One by one, the masses and religious leaders turned and walked away as Jesus came closer to the truth that he had to die for their salvation. Many of his followers were also offended by the truth and left him. Suddenly, Jesus found himself alone with the Twelve. Of them, he asked, "You do not want to leave too, do you?" Peter answered for them: "Lord, to whom shall we go? You have the words of eternal life. We believe and know that you are the Holy One of God" (John 6:67–69).

Later in the conference, another speaker from a worldwide ecumenical organization addressed the same body. In his message he urged Methodists to open their arms to non-Christian religions and join with them in a show of brotherhood. Theological differences and the claims of Christ were to be put aside for the sake of ecumenicity. Immediately, the stage was set for confrontation. Did we believe that Jesus Christ is the only hope for our salvation? Or were we parroting an old theme that was no longer relevant in the realities of a diverse religious world? In a press conference that echoed through the international media, I stood my ground, not with antagonism but with the confidence that Scripture had taught me right doctrine and had rebuked wrong doctrine. If the Scriptures are God-breathed and useful, there is no other choice.

Students of Scripture will also recall moments when the Word spoke to them about their behavior. In Paul's Epistle to the Corinthians, the apostle deals with a number of behavioral issues in the church, ranging from divisions over speaking in tongues to rationalizations about sexual immorality. While the issues are specific to the Corinthian Church, the principles are timeless. Sexual immorality, for instance, is as prevalent in our society today as it was in the corrupt city of Corinth. An hour before the television set watching daytime soaps or nighttime sitcoms leaves no doubt. Paul writes for us today when he says,

Do not be deceived: Neither the sexually immoral nor idolaters nor adulterers nor male prostitutes nor homosexual offenders nor thieves nor the greedy nor drunkards nor slanderers nor swindlers will inherit the kingdom of God. And that is what some of you are. But you were washed, you were sanctified, you were justified in the name of the Lord Jesus Christ and by the Spirit of our God.

1 Corinthians 6:9–11

All excuses for sexual immorality along with many other sins are lost. Whether by the action of sin or the attitude of acceptance, Christians who are washed, sanctified, and justified in the name of the Lord Jesus Christ and by the Spirit of God must separate themselves from all sexual immorality. The practice of sexual immorality is condemned and the attitude of tolerance cannot be condoned. With the Corinthians, Christians of the twenty-first century must say, "I stand corrected."

True to the God-breathed Scriptures, however, the apostle Paul goes beyond correction to instruction in right doing. After addressing each of the issues that divided the Corinthians, the Spirit of God inspired him to pull it all together in the monumental passage in 1 Corinthians 13, in which he shows his readers "the most excellent way" of love as the greatest of all gifts.

Can we expect to find similar tools for teaching in the Christian books we read? The answer is yes, if they are true complements to the Word of God. In Philip Yancey's book *What's So Amazing about Grace?* for example, he defines the doctrine of grace in clear biblical terms with illustrations from the life of Christ. Against that definition, he rebukes the many examples of "ungrace" that clutter the church and discourage believers. He then intertwines the biblical doctrine of grace with Christian behavior. Offering the biblical corrective for "ungrace," he engages the spirit of Jesus Christ for instruction in right doing. *What's So Amazing about Grace?* is true to the Word of God in text and tone. As well, it gives us useful tools for teaching, reproof, correction, and instruction in right doing. Consequently, the book is highly commended for all Christian readers.

Does This Book Contribute to Christian Maturity?

Once again, we stand amazed before timeless truth when we read that the end result of being schooled in the Scriptures is "that the man of God may be complete, perfectly equipped for every good work" (2 Tim. 3:17 Weymouth).

Here is proof that the Word of God has its own internal integrity. Contrary to many learning experiences that stop short of providing accountability for end results, the Scriptures boldly claim the outcomes of character ("a man of God"), competence ("equipped"), and consequences ("good work"). But there is more. The quality of these learning outcomes is intensified by descriptive words: "a man of God *complete*," "*perfectly* equipped," and for "*every* good work." No other teaching-learning experience, religious or secular, can make this claim. Maturity in the spirit of Jesus Christ is the promise for students of the Word.

In the depth of these words, we realize how far we fall short of the expectations and promises of God's teaching-learning process. Our shortcoming is no mystery. If we slight the reading of the God-breathed Word, the Holy Spirit is handicapped with dull tools for teaching, reproof, correction, and instruction in right doing. Why then should we be surprised that we fall short of godly character, feel spiritually incompetent in Christian witness, and fail at good works? The loop of learning takes us back to the basics. If we want the qualities associated with spiritual maturity, we must be avid readers of the God-breathed Word and serious students of Scripture.

Can we hold the same high expectations for Christian books? In this case, the first answer is no, because they cannot claim the God-breathed nature of Scripture. But if they are true to their purpose as commentaries on the

Word, we can expect Christian books to contribute to the qualities of godly character, spiritual competence, and beneficial consequences.

Charles Colson's autobiography, *Born Again,* illustrates how a Christian book complements the Word of God. Colson is introduced to us as the most ruthless of Watergate conspirators, known for hangman tactics such as letting political enemies "twist and turn in the wind." But when confronted by the gospel of Jesus Christ, he likens his conviction by the Holy Spirit to "being torpedoed." As we read his story, we feel as if we are witnessing a contemporary rerun of Saul's conversion on the Damascus road. The more we read, the more the Spirit of God speaks through the writing. We soon realize that we cannot hold the truth at arm's length. Identifying with Colson and entering into his experience leaves us gasping for spiritual breath.

After his conversion, Charles Colson could have spent his time enjoying the plaudits given to an "evangelical celebrity." Quite legitimately, he might also have envisioned himself as the "apostle to the powerful." After all, he had intimate acquaintance with the mightiest persons on earth. He chose, however, to ground his newfound faith in the study of the Word of God. Out of that experience, the Holy Spirit called him to return to the prisons and minister to the prisoners with whom he also identified. Later, he wrote the sequel to *Born Again* called *Life Sentence.* Today, we honor him as a man of God uniquely equipped to lead the good works of the worldwide ministry of Prison Fellowship. We can also commend Colson's books as contemporary complements to the Word of God. They inspire us to be godly, show us how the Holy Spirit equips us for ministry, and point us toward good works in Jesus' name.

In sum, we can judge Christian books by the extent to which they address the questions inferred in Paul's letter to Timothy when he describes the inspired Word—its nature, its function, and its results. Every time we read a Christian book, we should ask these questions:

- Is it true to the God-breathed Word?
    Is it true in text?
    Is it true in spirit?
- Is it useful for Christian teaching?
    Is it useful for teaching right doctrine?
    Is it useful for rebuking false doctrine?
    Is it useful for correcting wrong behavior?
    Is it useful for instruction in right doing?
- Does it contribute to Christian maturity?
    Does it inspire us to godly character?
    Does it equip us to live the Christian life?
    Does it lead us to good works?

To test this approach, think of a Christian book you have read recently and ask yourself these questions about the book. If your answers are affirmative, the book was well worth reading. If your answers are negative or you are uncertain how to answer, the book may not have been worth your time. Discerning readers will quickly know when a book addresses these questions and will be able to make a decision whether to continue reading, skim the text, or put it down.

4. Reading Christian Books as a Spiritual Discipline

Then Philip ran up to the chariot and heard the man reading Isaiah the prophet. "Do you understand what you are reading?" Philip asked. "How can I," he said, "Unless someone explains it to me?"

Acts 8:30–31

Whenever we think about improving our reading, increasing the speed at which we read often comes to mind. To be able to read more books within a limited amount of time is certainly a worthy goal. Speed-reading, however, can keep us from developing other more important reading skills. For one thing, speed-reading is a rigorous discipline that requires constant practice. Many people have attended speed-reading courses, learned the techniques, and then failed to follow through on them. For another thing, unless speed-reading results in better comprehension, we will be no better off than the hare in the well-known fable. Like the speedy hare, we may have superior reading speed, but those who take their time like the tortoise will win the race of comprehension. Of course, if we have the discipline to master both speed and comprehension, we will become world-class readers.

The truth is that most of us lack the time, money, or motivation to enroll in classes that promise to improve our reading speed and comprehension. Instead, we need some practical helps that we can apply during the course of our daily reading. If we can improve both the efficiency and effectiveness of our reading, we will get more from all the books we read. Christian books, in particular, deserve a quality read if they are to serve the purpose of helping us to understand the Christian faith and grow spiritually. Here are some helps for our consideration.

Let Christian Books Be Our Teacher

In a very real sense, we are students of the books we read. The author, though physically absent, is like a teacher giving a lecture or leading a discussion. We should choose books and authors, then, in the same way we select courses and teachers in school. We should read some books because they are like core courses that are required to understand a field of study. We should read others because they are like elective courses, which enrich a subject or address a personal interest. In either case, the key is to choose books that have something to teach us. Think of an author as an instructor who has knowledge or understanding that we do not have. The books we read should stretch us, not beyond our limits but in the same manner in which we progress through school. Introductory books come before advanced books, and required books come before electives.

In the field of theology, for instance, a beginning Christian reader will quickly become discouraged by Carl F. H. Henry's work in systematic theology entitled *God, Revelation, and Authority*. It is far better for such a person to start with John Stott's primer *Understanding the Christian Faith*, advance to J. I. Packer's *Knowing God*, add F. F. Bruce's *New Testament Theology*, and then if theology becomes a special interest, take on the meaty text of Henry's works. As a good student progresses from elementary to advanced levels of learning, a good reader progresses from elementary to advanced levels of reading.

Talk Back to Christian Books

In *How to Read a Book*, Mortimer Adler and Charles Van Doren describe the difference between an active and passive reader.[1] Using the analogy of a pitcher and a catcher in a baseball game, they suggest that the author is like a pitcher who throws fastballs, curves, and sliders to the reader or catcher. A passive reader is like a catcher who never returns the ball, while an active reader is one who fires the ball back in the form of questions that keep the game going and make the event exciting.[2]

The simplest question to ask is, "What do the terms mean?" If a Christian author uses the term *sin*, for instance, the meaning can vary from rebellion against God inherited from Adam to oppression created by an unjust social system against helpless people. Most authors define their terms. In some cases, however, the reader must determine definitions from inferences and innuendos. In either case, it is essential that author and reader work together on the same terms. Otherwise, like two ships passing in the night, the author and reader will glide past each other, ending up in different locations and with contradictory conclusions.

An active reader also looks for the topic sentence in each paragraph. Usually, these sentences come first and reveal the content of the paragraph. One of the advantages of using a yellow highlighter when we read is to note the topic sentence in each paragraph. Or if you prefer, use caret markings (^^) at the beginning and end of a topic sentence to set it off for future reference. By going back through the book and reading the marked topic sentences, a reader can usually see the outline of the book as a whole. Asking the question, "What are the topic sentences?" is the best way for a reader to unlock the secrets of the book.

Don't stop asking questions of the Christian books you read. From the beginning to the end, you must also ask, "What is this book about?" Every author tries to communicate a theme, advance an argument, or teach a lesson. The title might give us our first clue. If you pick up James Dobson's book *Dare to Discipline*, the title gives you a good idea about its content. But if you choose C. S. Lewis's *Screwtape Letters*, the title will provide no help. An active reader is always on the lookout for a major theme the author wants to communicate. Just as we can see the thread of God's redemptive plan running through the Old and New Testaments, we should also be able to discern a traceable thread weaving its way through the text of a good Christian book. A noteable example is Elton Trueblood's *Incendiary Fellowship*. From beginning to end, the theme of Spirit-filled passion enlivens the pages with the analogy of fire. Who can ever forget Trueblood's topic sentence for the entire book: "A good fire glorifies even its poorest fuel." In that sentence, every reader finds hope. The best of Christian books will do that for us.

Finally, we must ask, "What should I do with what I've read?" Like a good sermon, a good book leads us to a decision. Christian books, in particular, have an obligation to confront us with the claims of truth. We may be taken back to search the Word of God, driven to our knees, motivated to ask for forgiveness, or compelled to make a sacrifice of our self-interest. After reading John Perkins's *Let Justice Roll Down*, the question, "What should I do about it?" sticks in our mind until we repent and act. Lingering attitudes of discrimination toward minorities must be confessed and social systems of injustice condemned. To use an old-fashioned term, if a Christian book serves its purpose, it will end with an altar call.

Be a Disciplined Reader

Think of Christian reading as a spiritual discipline. Most often, we think of spiritual disciplines as practices such as fasting, Sabbath observance, or solitude. Dallas Willard, in his book *The Spirit of the Disciplines,* reminds us that there are also disciplines of engagement, such as Bible study, prayer, corporate worship, and small group ministries. Reading Christian books should be included among the disciplines of engagement. With the same discipline it takes to commit to Bible study or prayer, we should implement a plan for reading Christian books as a part of our daily schedule.

Start at the first of the year with a resolution to read. Although many New Year's resolutions are made to be broken, this one doesn't have to be. When it comes to reading, it is helpful to think ahead to the books we want to read and to schedule them in the year. The plan should begin with a list of books we want to read. Then, we need to ask, "How many books can we realistically read in a year?" If most Christian

59

books have approximately fifteen chapters and we read a chapter a day, the end result will be two books a month or twenty-four books a year! Such a plan is well within the scope of any average reader. So make a list of the books you want to read and leave room for new publications that hit the press. Just a chapter a day will make you an avid Christian reader.

Know Your Goal for Reading

Reading is not a one-dimensional exercise. We read different books for different purposes. If we know why we are reading as well as what we are reading, the experience will not only become more productive but also more meaningful.

Reading for Information

At the most basic level, we read to be informed. If it is true that we are in an age in which information has replaced money as the source of wealth and power, Christians, in particular, must be informed people. Otherwise, we too can become victims of spinmasters who manipulate minds and shape values. To avoid being duped by the half-truths of theological heresies that come in attractive media packages, we must be fully informed concerning the cardinal doctrines of the Christian faith. Books on apologetics, or "defenses of the faith," such as C. S. Lewis's *Mere Christianity*, Francis Schaeffer's *The God Who Is There*, Harry Blamires's *The Christian Mind*, and Josh McDowell's *Evidence That Demands a Verdict*, offer a strong and healthy diet of theological information.

Reading for Inspiration

Just as we often need to take a "Coke break" in a busy day, we also need a "pause that refreshes" when reading Christian books. If we read too much on one subject for a long period of time, the law of diminishing returns takes over. We become bored, inattentive, and finally exhausted.

Inspirational Christian books that are usually lighter in language and more free-flowing in style can give us the break we need. Autobiographies and biographies are especially good for letting us "get under the skin" of great saints and "feel the heartbeat" of our unsung heroes. Rather than struggling with the author's terms or searching for issues and arguments, we can read such a book as a drama that tugs at our emotions and lifts our soul. No one, for instance, can read Elisabeth Elliot's *Through Gates of Splendor* without weeping for our Christian martyrs or Billy Graham's *Just as I Am* without thanking God for anointing his servant.

Fiction may also fit into the category of inspirational reading. This is the case when the mind is set free to soar with the imagination of creative authors. C. S. Lewis is the acknowledged master of Christian fiction. Parents and children who read together The Chronicles of Narnia series will never forget the experience, and adults who read *The Great Divorce* will spend a lifetime debating the images of the fable.

Poetry tends to be the most neglected of inspirational Christian literature. Our high school English experiences should not continue to bias us. Calvin Miller's Singer Trilogy or Ruth Graham's *Sitting by My Laughing Fire* will rekindle the love for verse that we knew as children. The beauty, rhythm, and imagery of Christian poetry can cleanse our souls, enliven our minds, and set our spirits free.

Reading for Instruction

A majority of books sold in Christian bookstores are bought by mothers between the ages of 25 and 45 who are seeking help in raising children. Christian books, therefore, serve another important role. How-to books ranging from dating to parenting, personal growth to interpersonal relationships, and family budgeting to community evangelism all have a place on Christian family bookshelves. But keep in mind there is a risk in becoming too dependent on how-to books.

A young, single mother who was new to the faith became so intent on raising her children according to the formula given by one Christian author that neighbors said, "You could almost hear her turning the pages." Generally speaking, how-to books need to be balanced by other books on the same subject and complemented by teaching through the body of Christ.

Publishing Christian books for instruction may well be one of the most important ministries of the Christian press in the future. Currently, we are at a loss in knowing how to deal with the culture of violence that has been created in our society. Worse yet, the contamination of creeping secularism has blurred the line of sin and resulted in an evangelical culture of tolerance. If we are honest, we must confess that we are bewildered by questions about bringing up children in this society. What music should they hear? What web sites should they visit? What books should they read? What movies should they see? These are questions that will continue to plague us as the new world of media explodes upon us. Perhaps as never before, Christian families are at risk. We need guidance from authors who do not simply preach prohibitions but understand the complexity of the issues and deal forthrightly with them.

We also read Christian books for instruction when we are preparing to teach others. Whether a Sunday school teacher, small group leader, counselor, or speaker, each of us needs resources to enrich our instruction. In one way or another, each of us should cultivate our gifts and interests through Christian reading so that we can become specialists in a field. If we feel called, for instance, to a life of prayer, we should search out quality books on the subject. Included among these books are John Baillie's *Diary of Private Prayer*, E. M. Bounds's *Power through Prayer*, Rosalind Rinker's *Learning Con-*

versational Prayer, Jack Hayford's *Praying in the Spirit,* W. E. Sangster's *Teach Me to Pray,* Samuel Chadwick's *The Path of Prayer,* and E. Stanley Jones's *Abundant Living.* Imagine the strength and spirit of understanding we would bring to a conversation or a class on the subject of prayer if we had read these books.

The important point is that each of us has a gift or interest that we need to cultivate by reading. The apostle Paul wrote to the Corinthians, "But each man has his own gift from God; one has this gift, another has that" (1 Cor. 7:7). Later, in the same letter, he adds, "When you come together, everyone has a hymn, or a word of instruction, a revelation, a tongue or an interpretation. All of these must be done for the strengthening of the church" (1 Cor. 14:26). An insight from the books we read can be one of those gifts we bring to enrich and strengthen the body of Christ.

Reading for Interrogation

As our reading skills improve, our comprehension of the Christian faith can improve and our sensitivity to the mind of the Spirit can sharpen. We can also become more discerning as we read and more critical of what we read. Criticism, in this sense, is not cynicism. The attitude we bring to our reading makes all the difference. If we approach a Christian book with an attitude of distrust, the text will undoubtedly confirm our suspicions. If, however, we read a Christian book keeping an open mind as to whether the author is true to the faith, we can exercise the discerning mind of the Spirit in making a judgment on the text. Just as our faith should grow to maturity, our reading should develop to an advanced level. We need to progress from the milk-fed faith of babies to the "strong meat" of truth in our Christian reading as well as in our Christian understanding. Sooner or later, we should be able to distinguish the half-truths of modern heresies that would baffle a babe in Christ.

During the Gulf War of 1991, for instance, evangelical Christians rushed to bookstores to buy predictions that the battle of Armaggedon followed by the second coming of Christ was imminent. Of course, when the conflict ended without either event, the buying stopped and the books disappeared. But then prophets of doom reaped profits from the "millennial bug" as we turned the corner to the twenty-first century. Whether it is Y2K, UFO, or HIV, there is always an enterprising author who will make a profit on panic. Discerning Christian readers will follow the apostle's admonition to "test the spirits to see whether they are from God" (1 John 4:1). Rather than being swept up in the emotions of the moment, we must ask whether a book meets the test of the whole counsel of God. Then when the world panics and some flee to the mountains, with quiet confidence in the providence of God, we will go about our business, not oblivious to reality but calm in crisis.

In *How to Read a Book,* Adler and Van Doren use the term "analytical reading" to identify an advanced stage of critical reading. They give elaborate rules for working through a book analytically. Scholarly readers, in particular, can profit from their rules for finding out what a book is about, interpreting a book's contents, and criticizing a book for its communication of knowledge.[3]

Pigeonhole a book. In preparation for the work of analysis, Adler and Van Doren suggest that we begin by pigeonholing the book we are reading. Not all books should be read critically, and some books should be read more critically than others. Novels, for instance, are to be read less critically than expository works, which advance ideas and invite scrutiny. Likewise, theoretical books usually require more critical study than practical books that present methods of application. Among Christian books, works on theology, apologetics, and ethics invite critical reading more than devotionals, biographies, novels, and poetry.

X-ray the text. Once a book is pigeonholed, Adler and Van Doren suggest X-raying the text. This is the process of discovering the author's main theme and outlining the arguments that are advanced. They develop another elaborate process around the key questions, "What is the book about?" "What arguments are presented in detail?" "Are they true?" and "What of it?"

Come to terms with the author. After answering the above questions, we will begin to come to terms with the author. There is no shortcut to fair and honest criticism. Even though we may disagree with an author, we need to walk in his or her shoes before dismissing a book or repudiating its ideas. Working questions now include, "What are the ideas the author has advocated?" "Which of these ideas have been successfully defended and which have not?" Agree or not, we have given the author a fair hearing.

Make a fair judgment. As a result of these leading questions, the reader may critically conclude that the author is (1) uninformed, (2) misinformed, (3) illogical, or (4) incomplete in his or her ideas, issues, and arguments.

Follow the rules of etiquette. Even when we come to a negative conclusion about a book, Adler and Van Doren insist that we obey the "general maxims of intellectual etiquette" in our criticism:

- Do not criticize a book until you can say you understand the author's argument.
- Do not disagree contentiously.
- Demonstrate the difference between understanding and personal opinion by presenting good reasons for any critical judgment you make.

While these maxims are designed for all readers and all books, they are also basic for Christians who read Christian books analytically and make discerning judgments.

Be biblical in spirit. By the same process, we may also come to the conclusion that the author is informed, logical, and complete in presenting ideas and resolving issues. Then again, the process may lead us to suspend judgment until we deepen our analysis and read comparative books on the same subject. Criticism is never just an expression of personal opinion. Some standard of literary judgment is necessary. We have already presented the standard for Christian books: "Is this book true to the God-breathed Word?" Books of theology, apologetics, and ethics should especially be read critically with this question in mind. Otherwise, we will slip into the dangerous territory of interpreting the text and making critical conclusions based on our own biases.

As a case in point, the issue of abortion is at the center of controversy in our society. Among many Christians, a person's stand on abortion is a litmus test that divides family and churches. Some take a narrow pro-life stand that allows no exceptions. Some endorse a modified stand allowing for exceptions in cases of incest, rape, or threat to the life of the mother. And some move toward a position of choice in which the exceptions may include medical decisions for aborting a hopelessly impaired fetus during the early stages of pregnancy.

The point is that Christians need to be fully informed on these issues before jumping to judgment. Critical reading of more than one Christian author is required. Even though a reader may begin to read with the assumption that Scripture supports a certain pro-life stance, it is essential to know why other believers take another view. To be informed and complete in our moral conviction is part of being biblical. Equally important, however, to understand a contrary position without becoming contentious is consistent with the mind of the Spirit.

Discerning readers approach Christian books in the same way. While open to the truth, we must put our reading to the test against the whole truth of God's Word, the creeds of the church, and the history of God's people through the ages. To read Christianly and critically is not a contradiction in terms.

Reading for Integration

The highest level of Christian reading is to read for integration, or as Adler and Van Doren say, "to see things whole." They also refer to this stage of reading as "synoptical," the idea of looking through a lens and seeing things come together in one picture.[4] Immature readers of Christian books will take one book and view it as the summation of whole truth. More mature readers, however, will hold one book in abeyance until they have a chance to read other sources on the same subject. Then, always looking through the lens of the God-breathed Word, they put different viewpoints into the perspective of the whole, relate the viewpoints one to another, and draw them together into a composite conclusion without sacrificing the truth.

As an example of integrative or synoptical reading, I have recently read several books on the subject of holiness. As a young Christian, I was introduced to the doctrine from what is called a Wesleyan perspective, and more particularly, from a theology associated with the Holiness Movement. Accordingly, I was taught that holiness is a belief, experience, and practice defined as a second definite work of grace subsequent to the new birth and experienced at a specific point in time. In college and seminary, I read scores of books that defended this position from a scriptural viewpoint. Yet, other writers are quick to disagree. Although all orthodox Christian authors espouse "holiness" as a biblical mandate under God's command, "Be holy, for I am holy," the hows, whys, and wherefores of that experience are as diverse as the theological viewpoints from which the books are written.

My need for integrative reading came from interaction with Charles Colson. When we met in an airport one day, he told me he was writing *Loving God* on the subject of holiness.

Knowing of his Calvinist and Reformed orientation in theology, I said to him, partly in jest, "You can't write a book on holiness without letting a Wesleyan review it!"

"Good," he answered. "I'll send you the manuscript and let you make suggestions." When I read the manuscript, I saw that Colson's writing clearly reflected a viewpoint based on his solid understanding of Calvinist theology in the Reformed tradition. Without a doubt, the book had the strength of biblical belief, and its doctrine of holiness was focused on the sovereignty of God. But I felt as if it needed to be enlivened by the dynamic experience and disciplined practice of Wesleyan understanding. So I made several suggestions to Colson, which he adopted into his text and acknowledged in the credits.

From that experience, I realized that Christian believers of different traditions need to learn from each other. Therefore, I embarked on a journey of reading other authors on the subject of holiness. I read such books as Francis Shaeffer's *True Spirituality,* J. I. Packer's *Knowing God,* A. W. Tozer's *The Knowledge of the Holy,* R. C. Sproul's *The Holiness of God,* Vernon Grounds's *Radical Commitment,* and Jack Hayford's *Worship His Majesty.* Each of these authors addresses the question of biblical holiness from a different perspective. Each, therefore, contributed to my understanding of the doctrine and helped ground my belief in the Word of God. Although I still espouse my original position on the experience of holiness, it has been enlarged in scope and understanding. With genuine respect, I can appreciate the positions that other believers take on the subject and feel enriched by their contribution to my knowledge. For me, integrative reading of Christian books is the most rewarding experience of all.

From Discipline to Delight

When I speak, I often cite several Christian books in the course of my address. Afterward, people often ask me for advice on improving their reading. I answer, "Let me introduce you to my nightstand."

Years ago, I began placing five or six books on my nightstand next to the bed. The books represent a range of reading, and they usually include a work of fiction, a devotional classic, a book in my field of psychology, a contemporary Christian best-seller, a secular book on social issues, and an autobiography or biography of a great leader, secular or religious. From time to time, I insert a book of humor, poetry, or history for the sake of variation and balance. Each evening, then, before going to sleep, I spend twenty to thirty minutes reading one of these books. My choice of book depends on my mood, interest, or need at the time. Frankly, I am not ashamed to admit that I often fall asleep with an open book on my chest.

My nightstand reading gives rewarding results. In five or six weeks, I turn over the collection to keep my reading fresh and intriguing. By the time you read this book, for instance, I will have changed the books on my nightstand several times. At the risk of being dated, let me give you an idea of my current reading list. Looking over at my nightstand, I see these titles: John Grisham's best-selling novel *The Testament,* A. W. Tozer's *The Pursuit of God,* Dallas Willard's book of the year, *Divine Conspiracy,* C. S. Lewis's often read *The Great Divorce,* Jonathan Kozol's call for social compassion for impoverished children, *Amazing Grace,* and Howard Gardner's perspective on great leaders, *Leading Minds.*

Psychology has a law called "functional autonomy." According to this law, the habits we develop eventually become the drives that motivate us. The law can work for good or bad. In the case of Christian reading, it can only work for good. As we develop the habit of reading Christian books, we will find ourselves motivated to read, not just as a spiritual discipline but as a spiritual delight. Even now, as I look back at the list of books currently on my nightstand, I find myself energized by the thought of getting back to those books. The habit of reading is now a drive that motivates me. As part of my desire to be fully alive as a Christian in both mind and spirit, the discipline of reading has become sheer delight.

5. Planning a Personal Christian Library

Of making many books there is no end.
Ecclesiastes 12:12

Imagine that you are to be exiled all alone on a small, deserted island. You are given the privilege of taking your Bible and ten other books with you. Which ten books would you choose?

Answering that question is more than an intriguing party game. It addresses our acquaintance with the world of books, our areas of reading interest, and especially the values we hold. How many of the ten books would be religious and how many secular? How many would be classical and how many would be contemporary? How many would be theoretical and how many would be practical? How many would help us survive physically and how many would be geared to our intellectual and spiritual existence?

The Pyramid Principle

Behind these questions is a fundamental thought: You would want to choose books that you could read over and over again. Returning once again to *How to Read a Book,* Mortimer Adler and Charles Van Doren ask us to imagine our reading choices as a pyramid of books. At the broad base of the pyramid are millions of books that have been published that we will never read or need to read. If we read them at all, it would be for amusement or information.[1] Skimming would be quite adequate, and we would never return to these books because they add little to our knowledge or skills. Most contemporary novels fit this category. Exceptions for me would be Charles Sheldon's *In His Steps* and Fyodor Dostoyevsky's *Crime and Punishment.* After a gap of a few years, I enjoy reading them over again.

Above the base of the pyramid and at a second, narrower level are books that teach us how to read and how to live. Adler and Van Doren suggest that one book in a hundred might fit this category. "These are good books," they write, "the ones that were carefully wrought by their authors, the ones that convey to the reader significant insights about subjects of enduring interest to human beings."[2] Consequently, these books are worth reading once, analytically and in depth. When you have finished, you are grateful for their contribution to your understanding, but you know that you have grasped the essence of what the author has to offer. Occasionally, you might return to one of these books to locate a quotation or recapture an idea, but there is no need to reread it. In fact, if you return to one of these books and begin to reread it, Adler and Van Doren say that you will find "less there than you remembered."[3] Such a test will help you identify the books at this level.

For me, most of the best-sellers in Christian and secular literature fall into this category of books, which are worth one reading and contain a few good ideas. I read them to remain aware of what others are reading, but they don't qualify as top choices for my personal library. Usually, I skim them in the bookstore or check them out of the library. With one quick reading, they have served their purpose.

As the pyramid continues to rise and narrow again, Adler and Van Doren envision a much smaller number of books— less than one hundred—that cannot be exhausted by one reading. To distinguish this category of books, go back and begin to reread them. Instead of finding less than you remembered, you will find that the book has "grown with you." Perhaps this is only a way of testing our intellectual and spiritual growth over time, but it is also a credit to the depth of the book, whose treasures cannot be mined with one reading. The Word of God itself is our prime example. Job wrote about the depth of God's wisdom, which can never be exhausted by human searching. Each time we return to the Word of God, we find ourselves exclaiming, "I never saw that truth before." Though we sense that the Word has grown with us, in truth, we know that the Holy Spirit has enlightened our mind so that our spiritual growth is evident by new insights into God's revelation.

Using this criterion, we understand why so few books qualify for reading and rereading. Few authors have the depth of mind and spirit to bring us back to their books time and time again. Those who do are writers of Christian classics. Although St. Augustine's *Confessions* was written in the fourth century, the insights are timeless and the book is recognized in both the religious and secular worlds as a profound search into the deepest recesses of human personality and spiritual character. When rereading the book, one exclaims, "I never saw that truth before!"

Each of us has our own list of Christian classics. In my case, Dr. James F. Gregory, my spiritual and intellectual mentor, bequeathed to me in his will two books that had helped shape his great mind and gentle spirit. One was a leather-bound and gold-edged edition of Thomas à Kempis's *Imitation of Christ;* the other was C. S. Lewis's autobiography, *Surprised by Joy.* I have read these books several times and even now anticipate reading them again. Why? Because I grow with them and they grow with me each time I engage in communication with the authors.

Returning to the intriguing question, "If you were to be exiled all alone on a desert island, which ten books would you take with you?" we now know the basis for making this decision. We should select books that we can read more than once and that grow with us. No two persons will have the same list, and every one of us will find it difficult to limit our choices to just ten. Once we have made our selections, however, we will have reached the peak of the pyramid.

The Pyramid Plan

Using the pyramid principle as a general guideline, we can think more specifically about building a personal *Christian* library. Whereas the first pyramid we discussed included all the books that were ever printed, and our choices among those books depended on their value for teaching us how to read and how to live, our second pyramid involves only Christian books, and the choices we make depend on the value of the books for helping us understand the faith and grow spiritually.

The Pyramid Plan

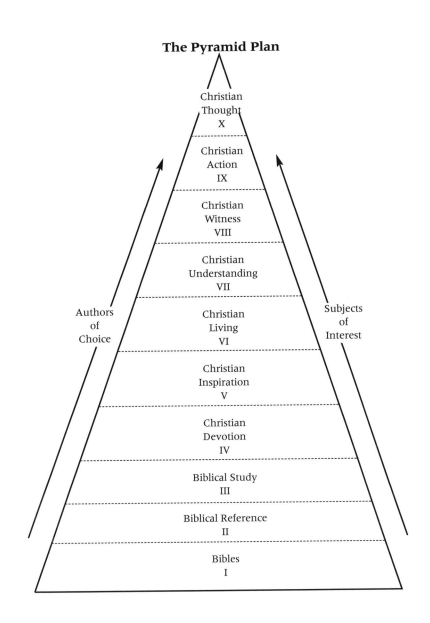

Christian
Thought
X

Christian
Action
IX

Christian
Witness
VIII

Christian
Understanding
VII

Authors
of
Choice

Christian
Living
VI

Subjects
of
Interest

Christian
Inspiration
V

Christian
Devotion
IV

Biblical Study
III

Biblical Reference
II

Bibles
I

The core of the pyramid is made up of ten tiers of books, beginning with the foundation of Bibles and rising to books that stretch the mind with Christian thought. The facia of the pyramid is made up of special collections that contain "authors of choice" and "subjects of interest." A brief description of each of these tiers in the pyramid along with a word on the finishing touches will give us a working plan for building a personal Christian library.

I. Bibles

The Scriptures are foundational to a Christian's personal library. Everyone has his or her favorite version, but one version or translation is not enough. At the minimum, we need two or three different Bibles to broaden our perspective on the Word. I rely heavily on the New International Version of the Thompson Chain Reference Bible, which has a thumb index in the pages to help me quickly find books of the Bible. My collection also includes the New King James Version, the Revised Standard Version, and the more contemporary translations of the Living Bible and the Message. Seldom do I refer to a text without comparing the language in a different version or translation. Invariably, I discover a deeper richness in the revelation.

II. Biblical Reference

When reading and studying Scripture, we should use reference sources such as biblical handbooks, commentaries, and concordances. Of course, there is no substitute for reading the Bible for ourselves and letting the Word speak to us through the mind of the Holy Spirit. But at the same time, multiple errors, ranging from theological heresy to behavioral sin, can result if we filter the Word through our own perceptions and senses. We need the check and balance of

Christian leaders and scholars who have commented on the meaning of the Word throughout history. Again, at the practical minimum, a personal Christian library should include a Bible dictionary, handbook, and concordance. *The Holman Bible Dictionary* is a standard reference source, and *Halley's Bible Handbook* is a proven text. We should choose a concordance that defines and locates common words throughout the Scriptures and matches our basic study Bible. In my case, the NIV Concordance, which complements my NIV version of the Thompson Chain Reference Bible, is an invaluable resource.

One set of biblical commentaries will bolster the reference section of a personal library. Choosing commentaries is a major decision because they range from intricate scholarly texts to expository helps for a layperson who teaches, writes, or counsels from Scripture. A centerpiece in my library is *The Communicator's Commentary* published by Word and edited by Lloyd Ogilvie. This is a biased choice because I wrote four of the commentaries in the collection. Pastors and laypeople, however, continue to compliment the series for its practical help in the exposition of Scripture. While I am not a biblical scholar in the strictest sense, my library also includes the Word Biblical Commentary series, which offers a more analytical and critical interpretation of the scriptural text. In between these two extremes, I find much help in the paperback collection of *The Bible Speaks Today*, with J. T. Motyer as Old Testament editor and John Stott as New Testament editor.

When all is said and done, our choice of a commentary series depends on our purpose in Bible study. If we want a resource for individual study and teaching, an expository commentary will serve us well as our first choice. When we advance in our study or teaching, a more analytical and critical commentary collection will add new depth to our understanding of the Word.

III. Biblical Study

Reading the Word of God is a discipline in itself. Certainly, there is value in reading the Bible for ourselves with an open mind and heart. We cannot forget, however, the story in Acts about the Ethiopian eunuch who was reading the Scriptures while traveling from Jerusalem back to his home country. Philip, the apostle, appeared in the chariot beside him and asked, "Do you understand what you are reading?" The Ethiopian answered, "How can I unless someone explains it to me?" (Acts 8:30–31). Philip, then, became his teacher, helping him understand what the Scriptures meant and how they applied to him as a person. The Ethiopian's belief and baptism attest to the value of that teaching-learning experience.

We, too, need some basic helps that teach us how to read, understand, and apply the Word of God to our life and experience. Years ago, Henrietta Mears wrote the book *What the Bible Is All About* as an outgrowth of her teaching through which she led many to Christ and nurtured them in the faith. More recently, Gordon Fee and Douglas Stuart have added another resource worthy of a place in our library under the attention-getting title *How to Read the Bible for All Its Worth.*

Serious readers of Scripture will also benefit from Robert Traina's *Methodical Bible Study* in which he teaches the principles of discovery when reading the Bible in English. His teaching reminds us again that the Scriptures are like a many faceted diamond. Each time we turn the gem into the light and see its beauty from another perspective, we realize that the Bible is the Book of Books because no matter how many times we read it, the truth can never be exhausted.

In addition to a book (or books) on how to study the Bible, we should consider separate studies of the Old and New Testaments. Usually, these books resemble classroom textbooks, but not in the sense that we need a professor to help us understand what we read. *The Message of the New Testament* by

F. F. Bruce and *Old Testament Introduction* by William Lasor, David Hubbard, and Frederic Bush are basic books for advanced readers.

Keep in mind that a personal Christian library cannot be built by formula. Books on Bible study are essential to the library, but each category contains biblically sound and readable books from which we may choose. Pastors, teachers, and friends who are readers are a ready source for good recommendations. By following the guidelines in the chapters "How to Choose a Christian Book" and "How to Judge a Christian Book," however, we can make the final choice.

IV. Christian Devotion

The natural step after Bible study is the category of devotional books, which assist us in our spiritual development. Three categories make up this section of our collection. First, there are books for daily devotions throughout the year. Although not marked out for 365 days of reading, Thomas à Kempis's all-time classic *The Imitation of Christ* lends itself to daily reading. For depth of spiritual insights, the volume still stands alone. In a more contemporary setting, Oswald Chambers's *My Utmost for His Highest* has become one of the most widely read devotionals, helping to satisfy the thirst for spirituality and hunger for holiness among Christians. Earlier generations read Mrs. C. E. Cowman's *Streams in the Desert* and E. Stanley Jones's *The Way* in response to those same needs. Each and all of these books are worthy additions to a personal Christian library.

Books on prayer represent the second category in the devotional section of a library. Several books on prayer are highly recommended for Christian readers. Among these, *A Diary of Private Prayer* by John Baillie, *With Christ in the School of Prayer* by Andrew Murray, *The Practice of the Presence of God* by Brother Lawrence, *Conversing with God* by Rosalind Rinker, and *Prayer: Finding the Heart's True Home* by Richard Foster are first choices for a smaller, personal library.

Daily devotions and spiritual discipline are like two sides of the same coin. Without one, we don't have the other. In recent years, many people have reemphasized spiritual discipline as essential to Christian life in an undisciplined age. Once again, we have multiple choices for books in this field. Reaching back a generation or two, we are privileged to find Dietrich Bonhoeffer's *Cost of Discipleship*. Bonhoeffer wrote his book as a Christian struggling to be faithful to his Lord during Hitler's regime in Nazi Germany. Even though we may have the freedom of democracy, Bonhoeffer's insights will challenge and convict us. Also from a past generation are the still-timely insights of A. W. Tozer's *Pursuit of God* and W. E. Sangster's *Path to Perfection*. To the credit of our contemporary authors, we have potential classics in Richard Foster's *Celebration of Discipline,* Dallas Willard's *The Spirit of the Disciplines,* and Eugene Peterson's *A Long Obedience in the Same Direction.* Two or more of these books, both classical and contemporary, will make the library section entitled "Christian Devotion" commended to all.

V. Christian Inspiration

Each of us needs models and mentors for the development of our Christian life. Although there is no substitute for having direct contact with a mentor, the books we read can also be influential in shaping our character and our conduct. As a boy, for instance, my father was my model and mentor. But I also discovered other heroes through autobiographies and biographies. Through my reading, I shared the adventures of Daniel Boone, the wisdom of Abraham Lincoln, and the vision of Christopher Columbus. During my high school years, I was profoundly influenced by Dag Hammarskjöld, as he shared his faith in the difficult role of secretary general of the United Nations in *Markings*. As a budding journalist, I identified with Eric Sevareid's story of his life under the title *Not So Wild a Dream*. Slowly, but surely, I became an avid collector and reader of autobiographies and biographies. It was Elton Trueblood, however, who taught me the value of entering into the sainted lives of Christian men and women who showed how to live and lead in times past. He recommended that I read St. Augustine's *Confessions* and Blaise Pascal's *Pensees*. Later, his recommendation was reinforced when another of my mentors, Dr. James F. Gregory, president of Spring Arbor College, bequeathed to me *Surprised by Joy*, the autobiography of C. S. Lewis.

The shelf of autobiographies and biographies in my personal library now holds a special collection for me. That shelf contains the most influential books of my life: *Here I Stand* by Roland Bainton, *This Freedom—Whence?* by John Wesley Bready, *A Song of Ascents* by E. Stanley Jones, *Through Gates of Splendor* by Elisabeth Elliot, *Just as I Am* by Billy Graham, and, of course, *While It Is Day* by Elton Trueblood. These books have permitted me to identify so completely with great servants of God that my own Christian character has been shaped and shamed by them. While recognizing that autobiographies and biographies are a highly personal choice, no library should be without at least a few of them. For inspiration in reading, they are essential.

VI. Christian Living

Our faith is more than belief and experience. We must also demonstrate our faith in the bump and grind of daily life and relationships. No one claims that living a Christian life is easy. In fact, C. S. Lewis said that his difficulties began when he became a Christian. We identify with this truth and seek help from books on such crucial topics of Christian living as personal growth, interpersonal relationships, sex, marriage, and family matters. It is no surprise that books in this category have made up the majority of sales of Christian publications in the past three or more decades. A personal Christian library should reflect this need, but on a highly selective basis related specifically to issues with which we must deal. Still, there is a core of basic books in this category to which we can turn for help time and time again.

Since the introduction of relational theology in the 1960s, books on personal growth for Christians have flourished in the marketplace. *The Taste of New Wine* by Keith Miller led the way and is still relevant today. Other books of note that address Christian living and personal growth include *Discovering God's Will in Your Life* by Lloyd Ogilvie and *Ordering Your Private World* by Gordon MacDonald. Advanced reading will take us to two classics that should be in our libraries: *The Four Loves* by C. S. Lewis and *The Meaning of Persons* by Paul Tournier.

A word of caution is needed as we read and buy books that address personal and interpersonal issues. Many authors have become enamored with the findings of modern psychology, theories of human development, and techniques of psychotherapy or counseling. Christians are often tempted to buy into these popular ideas and apply them directly to personal Christian growth without checking the theories against biblical theology. For example, many Christian books extol the virtues of "self-actualization" in personal development. Although the teachings of Jesus include the promise of "self-actualization," it is always combined with the paradoxical idea of "self-sacrifice." Without applying this biblical balance, supposedly "Christian" books can actually be vehicles for teaching the heresy of half-truth. The key is to choose books in this field that begin with biblical truth and build on that foundation rather than use the Scriptures to sanctify human theory.

Christian books address the full range of family relationships, from dating to divorce and from birth to death. If the volume of books in this field is indicative of our needs, the Christian family is one of the most beleagured of our primary institutions. Beginning with such a fundamental text as *Sex for Christians* by Lewis Smedes, following through with a help such as *How to Lead Your Child to Christ* by Luis and Pat Palau, helping young people in dating by reading *I Loved a Girl* by Walter Trobisch, advising newly married couples with *Letters to Karen* and *Letters to Philip* by Charlie Shedd, addressing married life with Elizabeth Achtemeier's *The Committed Marriage*, and taking on the task of Christian parenting with the counsel of James Dobson in *Dare to Discipline*, we see the range of reading that is before us. These books, however, represent a solid foundation for family development.

As startling as it may seem, statistics show that Christians are no more exempt from personal and interpersonal problems than their secular counterparts. This reality accounts for the fact that Christian buyers have made best-sellers out of such writings as *Healing for Damaged Emotions* by David Seamands, *Forgive and Forget* by Lewis Smedes, *Where Is God When It Hurts?* by Philip Yancey, and *Rebuilding Your Broken World* by Gordon MacDonald. Many more biblically and psychologically sound volumes are available to help us with individual problems. *When Our Parents Need Us Most*, a book that I wrote for children who are care givers for elderly parents, is an example of a book that meets a special need in family relationships. Together, through our reading, Christians can communicate with each other and learn from the experience of others.

VII. Christian Understanding

Spiritual growth is a matter of mind as well as heart. In 1 Peter 1:13 we read, "Prepare your minds for action." Mental preparation, therefore, is another spiritual discipline that we must cultivate. Although we may resist the exercise, unless our minds are stretched, we will not grow. In this section of books in our personal library, therefore, we need to include readable works on biblical theology that help us understand what we believe and companion texts on church history that tell us how we relate to Christians through the ages.

A solid cornerstone for the section on Christian theology is made up of John Stott's *Basic Christianity*, J. B. Phillips's *Your God Is Too Small*, and A. W. Tozer's *The Knowledge of the Holy*. Philip Yancey has also given sound and readable theology in his books *The Jesus I Never Knew* and *What's So Amazing about Grace?* Maturing Christians will not shy away from time-tested works on theology such as *Knowing God* by J. I. Packer, *The Cross of Christ* by John Stott, and *The Divine Conspiracy* by Dallas Willard.

The subject of church history may conjur up the old idea from high school that history is as dry as dust. It need not be. In fact, we need to remember the countering truth that those who refuse to learn from history are condemned to repeat it. Contemporary Christians whose faith is contaminated by the secular influence of self-interest may especially need the corrective of church history. Bruce Shelley meets that need in the content of his book *Church History in Plain Language*. After reading this book, many will discover an unexpected thirst to read more. Mark Noll's *Turning Points*, Donald Dayton's *Discovering an Evangelical Heritage*, Earle Cairn's *Christianity through the Centuries*, and especially Kenneth Latourette's *Christianity through the Ages* will not only satisfy that thirst but add to the motivation to keep reading. Until we know from where we have come, we cannot know where we are going.

Our Christian understanding would be deficient without a perspective on the nature of the church and the meaning of worship. Because both of these areas are subjects of debate today, we need a biblically based outlook on these issues. Books on the church, or ecclesiology, include *The Community of the King* by Howard Snyder, *The Body* by Charles Colson, and *The Company of the Committed* and *The Incendiary Fellowship* by Elton Trueblood. To catch a glimpse of the growing church today and the emerging church of the future, we can read *The Purpose-Driven Church* by Rick Warren and *A Church for the Twenty-first Century* by Leith Anderson.

Changes in Christian worship have been even more dramatic than changes in the church itself. The tension between traditional and contemporary patterns is so great that some observers allude to "worship wars." By reading such books as Robert Webber's *Worship Is a Verb*, Jack Hayford's *Worship His Majesty*, Warren Wiersbe's *Real Worship*, and Marva Dawn's *Reaching Out without Dumbing Down*, we can contribute to the solution rather than the problem. Because our worship tells the world what we believe about God, a personal Christian library is not complete without books that guide us to the truth.

VIII. Christian Witness

Up to this point in our pyramid plan, the recommended books have focused on personalized aspects of Christian growth and understanding. Although the internal development of Christian character is a never-ending task, it must not become an end in itself. Following the command of Christ and his example to us, we are to "give ourselves away" by introducing others to our Savior and sacrificially serving their needs.

A personal library should reflect that outward thrust, beginning with our witness to the world. Although Paul Little's life was cut short by a tragic accident at the peak of his ministry, he left us the legacy of his book *How to Give Away Your Faith*, which should be an anchor in this section. Rosalind Rinker also gave us encouragement for personal evangelism in her book *You Can Witness with Confidence*.

To see the Great Commission in full scope, add Robert Coleman's *Master Plan of Evangelism* along with John Stott's *Christian Mission in the Modern World*. Other authors have added a contemporary touch to witnessing based on proof of effective results. Examples include Bill Hybels and Mark Mittelberg's *Becoming a Contagious Christian*, James Kennedy's *Evangelism Explosion*, and Joe Aldrich's *Lifestyle Evangelism*. Likewise, George Hunter's book *How to Reach Secular People* customizes Christian witness to the realities of the age in which we live.

IX. Christian Action

An effective Christian witness must be both personal and social. Throughout the history of the church, there has always been tension over a Christian's role and responsibility as a social witness, especially when government and politics are involved. The tension mounts as new moral issues of a rapidly changing world crowd the social agenda. More often than not, we find ourselves reacting to the items on this new agenda rather than anticipating them. The lag between practice and principle will inevitably continue in the future with the increasing speed of technological advancements and social change. Still, we cannot ignore our responsibility as believers to remain alert to these issues, seek biblical solutions, and take risks for the causes of justice and mercy.

More than fifty years ago, Carl F. H. Henry led evangelical Christians back into the social arena with his book *The Uneasy Conscience of Modern Fundamentalism*. Sherwood Wirt urged another positive step forward with *The Social Conscience of the Evangelical*, and David Moberg, the sociologist, called us to biblical social action when he took the title for his book *Inasmuch: Christian Social Responsibility in the Twentieth Century* from Matthew 25, which portrays the final judgment when we are called to accountability for our ministry to the poor, the prisoner, and the stranger among us.

Later volumes in Christian social action are equally memorable. In the midst of racial crisis, the legendary John Perkins wrote *Let Justice Roll Down*. In response to our Western affluence, Ronald Sider chose the convicting title *Rich Christians in an Age of Hunger*, and when the abortion issue heated up,

Francis Schaeffer and C. Everett Koop toured the nation to promote their book *Whatever Happened to the Human Race?* In more general terms, but still pungent in truth, Rebecca Manley Pippert urged Christians to come *Out of the Salt Shaker and into the World,* Tom Sine built his appeal for Christian social action on a biblical analogy in *The Mustard Seed Conspiracy,* and Tony Campolo addressed the conscience of Christian youth with his book *You Can Make a Difference.*

There is no lack of books on Christian social action, nor is there a lack of controversy surrounding them. In this section of our library, we need a basic volume or two on Christian social responsibility that also has biblical credibility. We need to learn that there are two sides to Christian social action: justice, which usually involves the legislative, legal, and executive systems of society, and mercy, which most often involves relief from suffering for individuals and groups. The truth may be difficult to hear, but we cannot ignore the social facet of our faith. Rather than limiting our reading to books with which we agree, we will find that mind-stretching and soul-searching volumes will both broaden our perspective and keep us humble.

X. Christian Thought

As the pyramid plan unfolds and rises, the subject matter of the books may seem more complex and intimidating. This may be true of many books with ominous titles that address such subjects as apologetics and ethics. A number of books have been written, however, that a lay reader can both read and understand. These books, too, are essential for a personal Christian library because they represent three important dimensions of faith: embracing our faith within a thoroughly Christian view, defending our faith in everyday conversation, and affirming our faith in moral decisions and ethical conduct.

When seeking to understand and embrace the Christian worldview, there is no better book than Harry Blamires's *The Christian Mind*. For those who might think that biblical faith is strong on things of the Spirit but weak on things of the mind, the corrective is John Stott's pocket classic *Your Mind Matters*. Other books worthy of a place on our library shelves are Mark Noll's *The Scandal of the Evangelical Mind*, Josh McDowell's *Evidence That Demands a Verdict*, and Greg Boyd's *Letters from a Skeptic*.

In the field of ethics, lay readers will find practical application to daily living in Lewis Smedes's *Mere Morality* and Richard Mouw's *Uncommon Decency*.

Standing alone at the peak of the pyramid in the section on Christian thought is C. S. Lewis's *Mere Christianity*. Close behind is Elton Trueblood's *A Place to Stand*. Even though these books were published in the second half of the twentieth century, they have already stood the test of time and have lasting value. Whenever the best books of the twentieth century are mentioned, *Mere Christianity* is at the top of the list. Trueblood's book, as well, is recommended as a definitive statement of faith.

Finishing the Pyramid

Like the ancient pyramids of Egypt, our pyramid needs the finishing touch of smooth facia over the rough building blocks of stone. "Authors of choice" and "subjects of interest" give our library the finishing touch of our own personal signature.

Authors of choice represent a special collection of books that especially resonate with our own mind and heart. Like the signature of an artist on a painting, these books put a personal stamp of character on our library. Each of us has had the experience of reading a book that especially contributed to our spiritual growth and shaped our Christian character. In response to that book, we vow to read other books by that author. As a result, a special collection is born. We search for other books by the author, buy them whenever possible, read them more than once, and quote from them freely. Authors of choice can be detected in the sermons of preachers, the lessons of teachers, and conversations with friends.

Earlier I mentioned my collection of books by C. S. Lewis, Elton Trueblood, and Henri J. M. Nouwen. If asked the question, "Which Christian authors have had the greatest influence on your life?" I would name these three. Lewis's autobiography, *Surprised by Joy,* set the tone for my Christian life, Trueblood's *The New Man for Our Time* provided me with a model for a Christian scholar, and Nouwen's *In the Name of Jesus* showed me how the spirit of Jesus Christ defines the character of Christian leadership. Books by these three authors are the signature collections in my personal library.

Authors of choice often serve as conversation starters among Christian readers. Just the other day, for instance, a retired businessman drove me to the airport. We immediately found that books were a common interest, and within minutes we knew we were brothers in Christ. A chord was struck at the mention of Henri Nouwen's name. From there, we talked about spiritual insights we had gleaned from Nouwen's writings. Too soon, we arrived at the airport, shook hands, and vowed to keep in touch. Within a matter of days, we had exchanged mail. I sent him a quote from Nouwen that he had lost, and in turn, he sent me a copy of a Nouwen monograph I had missed. An author of choice led to a meaningful conversation and a continuing relationship.

Every Christian reader will benefit from collecting books that speak to subjects of interest and put a finishing touch on his or her personal library. It is good to be a generalist when it comes to reading, but it is also good to be a specialist in certain subjects so that we can contribute the gift of our understanding in communication with the body of Christ or in witness to others. A subject of particular interest may come from any one of the sections of the pyramid. From prayer to ethics and from Bible study to church history, our conversations are enlivened and our classrooms are enriched when each member of the body brings the gift of a special perspective to the table.

You can now build your pyramid of books. By selecting volumes for each tier in the structure, your library will be under way. A library developed according to the pyramid principle of choosing books that you would want to read more than once and designed according to the pyramid plan of selecting books in a range of subjects will give you a well-rounded resource for Christian reading. Most important, your personal library will contribute to the singular goal of Christian reading: that we will be men and women of God, perfectly equipped for every good work.

6. Introducing a Three-Year Christian Reading Plan

Fix these words of mine in your hearts and mind. . . . Teach them to your children. . . . Write them on the doorframes of your houses and on your gates, so that your days and the days of your children may be many in the land.

Deuteronomy 11:18–21

A ssume that a new believer asks you, "What Christian books should I read to grow spiritually?" Or if you are a parent, assume that your high school son or daughter asks you, "What books do you recommend I read to understand the Christian faith?"

A Lifelong Vision

These questions have followed me for years. In the 1960s, as I watched the blossoming growth of the Christian book industry, I thought about these questions. In the 1970s, when Christian publishers produced one out of every three books in the market, the questions came back with force. No one can doubt the power of the press when it comes to Christian publications, but one can legitimately wonder, "Are Christians reading more but discerning less?" Even more specifically, "Is their reading leading them to Christian understanding and spiritual growth?"

Red warning flags went up in the decades that followed as books on pop religious psychology, doomsday prophecy, and apocalyptic fiction topped the best-seller lists. It appeared that market-driven forces more than biblically based judgment influenced the reading choices of many Christians, especially new believers and searching youth.

Red flags flew again when polls showed that many Christians fail basic tests of biblical beliefs, differ little in attitude from their secular counterparts, and tend to remain immature in their faith after conversion. While reading Christian books is not the only answer to these problems, it can be an important tool of Christian discipline and development.

All of these concerns were reinforced by personal visits to Christian homes when I was a college, university, and seminary president. As I mentioned earlier, I made it a point to note the periodicals in the magazine racks and the books on the shelves of our Christian homes. A Bible was almost always present along with a denominational or interdenominational magazine and occasionally, a popular Christian book.

Devotional books were rare, collections of Christian books were rarer still, and Christian classics were almost nonexistent. Soon, the lingering questions of the past took on a new urgency as I asked myself, "What do new believers read to grow spiritually?" and "What do our children read to understand the Christian faith?"

Through the years, I looked wistfully at the *Great Books of the Western World*, a collection that serves as the centerpiece on the shelves of our family room. Years ago, Robert Maynard Hutchins, the boy wonder president of the University of Chicago, created an experimental undergraduate curriculum around the reading of the great books. He and his colleague, Mortimer Adler, developed a process for selecting the greatest books of the Western world for that curriculum. Volumes chosen had to be universal in truth, timeless in value, and literary in quality.

Consequently, they chose fifty-four books ranging in subject matter from philosophy to fiction and by date from Plato to Tolstoy. They also provided a reading plan for the great books and a cross-reference guide for tracing ideas throughout the books. Although I am still far behind in my reading of this collection, the introduction to great ideas and great authors through *The Great Books* has been a learning experience as valuable as my undergraduate education.

Each time I look at the *Great Books of the Western World* on my bookshelf, I envision a similar collection of "great books of the Christian faith" serving as the centerpiece for the shelves of our living rooms, family rooms, and dens in Christian homes.

At the end of the twentieth century my interest in the idea peaked when I saw so many lists and displays of the "greatest," "best," and "classic" books of the last one hundred years. Evangelical Christian publishers have followed suit with various collections, such as Christian classics through history, special subjects of contemporary interest, and favorites of prominent evangelical Christian leaders. A void still exists, however, around the specific questions of a new believer, "What Christian books should I read to grow spiritually?" and a young member of the family who inquires of parents, "What books do you recommend I read to understand the Christian faith?" Behind each of these questions is the common concern that Christians of the twenty-first century remain true to biblical faith in belief and practice as well as experience.

In response to these questions, I found myself moving from interest to impatience and from inspiration to implementation for a Christian three-year reading plan. For me, it was an idea whose time had come.

The Vision Becomes a Plan

Simply put, the plan was to develop a process for selecting thirty-six books that had been published in the last fifty years, were potential classics, and would assist lay readers in understanding the Christian faith and growing spiritually. These thirty-six books would comprise a three-year plan that would encourage the laity to follow a comprehensive and progressive schedule of Christian reading. Admittedly, the time limit of the last half century ruled out many Christian classics that had been tested over the centuries. They deserve a collection of their own on the shelves of Christian family libraries. To meet the purpose of this project, however, I made the decision to select more contemporary books that would appeal to the average lay reader.

I began the process of selection by searching through literature for best-sellers, award winners, and recommended books from the past fifty years. Out of this search, I came up with a preliminary list of 120 books. Fifteen persons whom I knew to be avid and discerning readers of Christian literature agreed to review the list and provide reasons for making additions and deletions. Based on their responses, I compiled an expanded survey form and sent it to seventy-eight prominent Christian authors and leaders, requesting their top three choices of books in various categories and inviting them to recommend other books for the top spots. The respondents were asked to imagine a new believer or a young member of the family asking them the question, "What books would you recommend I read to help me understand the Christian faith and grow spiritually?"

Selections by the respondents also had to be made according to these criteria:

Biblical credibility. The content of the book is true to Scripture and consistent with the statement of faith in the Lausanne Covenant.

Lay readability. The book can be read and comprehended by a layperson with the reading skills of a high school graduate who is motivated to develop skills for more advanced reading.

Literary quality. The style of writing, depth of thought, timelessness of truth, and universality of application qualify the book as a potential classic to be read and reread again and again.

Developmental value. The book is especially conducive to understanding the Christian faith and nurturing spiritual growth.

Responses came from 50 percent of the Christian authors and leaders who were invited to participate. Their top three choices and alternative recommendations were then submitted to a selection committee of eleven well-known Christian authors to narrow the list down to thirty-six books. Members of the selection committee were the following:

Leith Anderson, senior pastor, Woodale Community Church

Jill Briscoe, author and speaker

Maxie Dunnam, president, Asbury Theological Seminary

Ted Engstrom, president emeritus, World Vision

Vernon Grounds, president emeritus, Denver Theological Seminary

Jack Hayford, senior pastor, The Church on the Way

Jay Kesler, president emeritus, Taylor University

James Earl Massey, dean emeritus, Anderson Theological Seminary

Rebecca Manley Pippert, author

Rick Warren, senior pastor, Saddleback Community Church

David McKenna, chair and general editor

The Plan Becomes a Reality

With the continuing counsel of the distinguished selection committee, the final list of thirty-six books took shape. Three editorial decisions governed the final selection process: (1) The books should be readable for laypersons; (2) the list should contain only one book per author, except for C. S. Lewis; and (3) the list should progress from introductory to more advanced writing. Accordingly, following is the list of thirty-six volumes we propose for a progressive three-year reading plan.

As you review the plan, you will see a specific design. First, the plan is divided into one-year segments with books scheduled for reading in each month of the year. You may start to read the books at any time of the year, but whenever you start, it is recommended that you begin with the introduc-

	Year 1 Introductory Reading	Year 2 Enriched Reading	Year 3 Advanced Reading
January	*My Utmost for His Highest,* Oswald Chambers	*Power through Prayer,* E. M. Bounds	*A Diary of Private Prayer,* John Baillie
February	*Through Gates of Splendor,* Elisabeth Elliot	*Just as I Am,* Billy Graham	*Surprised by Joy,* C. S. Lewis
March	*Understanding the Bible,* John Stott	*What the Bible Is All About,* Henrietta Mears	*How to Read the Bible for All Its Worth,* Gordon Fee and Douglas Stuart
April	*Celebration of Discipline,* Richard Foster	*The Spirit of the Disciplines,* Dallas Willard	*The Cost of Discipleship,* Dietrich Bonhoeffer
May	*How to Give Away Your Faith,* Paul Little	*The Master Plan of Evangelism,* Robert Coleman	*Out of the Salt Shaker and into the World,* Rebecca Manley Pippert
June	*How to Lead Your Child to Christ,* Luis and Pat Palau	*Dare to Discipline,* James Dobson	*I Married You,* Walter Trobisch
July	*The Jesus I Never Knew,* Philip Yancey	*Knowing God,* J. I. Packer	*Mere Christianity,* C. S. Lewis
August	*Worship His Majesty,* Jack Hayford	*Real Worship,* Warren Wiersbe	*Worship Is a Verb,* Robert Webber
September	*Healing for Damaged Emotions,* David Seamands	*Forgive and Forget,* Lewis Smedes	*The Meaning of Persons,* Paul Tournier
October	*Let Justice Roll Down,* John Perkins	*Rich Christians in an Age of Hunger,* Ronald Sider	*The Politics of Jesus,* John Yoder
November	*Church History in Plain Language,* Bruce Shelley	*Turning Points,* Mark Noll	*Here I Stand,* Roland Bainton
December	*The Body,* Charles Colson	*The Company of the Committed,* Elton Trueblood	*The Christian Mind,* Harry Blamires

Introducing a Three-Year Christian Reading Plan

❖

97

tion *How to Read a Christian Book* and continue to follow the curriculum through the ensuing months.

Second, the books in the first year are intended to introduce the beginning reader to each of the twelve subjects in the library (discussed below). In the second year, then, the subject areas are enriched, and in the third year, they are addressed in more depth and detail. There is no lag in the quality of writing or content among the three years. All books meet the stringent criteria of selection: biblical credibility, layperson readability, literary quality, and developmental value.

Third, the plan allows for variety in the reading schedule during the year. After starting with a devotional classic early in the year, foundational reading continues until the summer months, when the choices are intended for more relaxed reading in discretionary or vacation time. In the fall, the schedule returns to books that apply the faith in practice. Each year concludes, then, with a book already acknowledged as a classic in Christian literature.

Fourth, within the plan itself, you will detect twelve subject areas. Following, the twelve subjects are identified with an example of a book on each one:

1. Bible study
   What the Bible Is All About, Henrietta Mears
2. Devotion and prayer
   My Utmost for His Highest, Oswald Chambers
3. Spiritual discipline
   Celebration of Discipline, Richard Foster
4. Theology
   Mere Christianity, C. S. Lewis
5. The church and worship
   The Company of the Committed, Elton Trueblood
6. Church history
   Church History in Plain Language, Bruce Shelley

7. Autobiography/biography
   Through Gates of Splendor, Elisabeth Elliot
8. Evangelism and missions
   The Master Plan of Evangelism, Robert Coleman
9. The family
   Dare to Discipline, James Dobson
10. Christian living
    Healing for Damaged Emotions, David Seamands
11. Social issues
    Let Justice Roll Down, John Perkins
12. Apologetics/ethics
    The Christian Mind, Harry Blamires

Notably absent are books of fiction and poetry. Although these books are highly recommended for the cultivation of imagination and inspiration, the decision was made to build the library on other subjects, with fiction and poetry as complementary reading.

Books on such popular subjects as prophecy, leadership, and gender roles along with the writings of authors who present a specific theological or denominational perspective have also been excluded. Many of the books in these categories are worth reading, but due to the limited number of volumes in our three-year plan, it is virtually impossible to include some and not others. As much as we could, books were chosen for biblical soundness without a dominant slant in one theological direction or another.

Reality Becomes Opportunity

Many hints and helps have already been given for reading a Christian book. All of these suggestions apply to the books in the three-year plan. Now, however, it is time to go directly to the list itself and begin reading. A simple, ten-step strategy will help you get started.

Step 1: Meet the Author

Each of the books in the three-year reading plan will more than likely contain a brief biographical introduction to the author. Reading the biographical brief lets you "shake hands" with the author as a person, a writer of note, and a thoughtful leader of the Christian community. As you read the book, assume that you are entering into a conversation with a friend from whom you can learn much as you grow in mind and spirit.

Step 2: Grasp the Thought

Many books contain a preface written by the author. Often we skip these introductory pages and go directly to the text. When we do, we miss the opportunity to enter into the mind of the author. In a well-written preface, the author explains the reasons for writing the book, reveals its theme, and perhaps explains what he or she hopes the reader will learn. Discerning readers will not skip the author's preface. They know that once they enter into the mind of the writer and grasp the thought behind the book, they gain a perspective that helps them understand the rest of the book.

Step 3: Ponder These Questions

After reading the chapter "Judging a Christian Book," readers should have in the back of their minds these three primary questions:

1. Is the book true to the inspired Word of God?
2. Is it useful for Christian teaching?
3. Does it contribute to Christian maturity?

By asking these questions before we begin to read, we create a framework for judging what we read. After reading several chapters, we should ask the questions again to assess whether we should continue reading. Finally, after completing the book, the questions provide a standard for judging the quality of the book. Of course, more specific questions should be asked of each book due to differences in subject matter, but the above three questions apply to every book that attempts to provide a Christian message.

Step 4: Find a Friend

While each of us knows the value of solitude as we read, we also know the enhanced value of reading a book with someone. The person becomes our corrector, our confidant, and our encourager as we talk through the ideas of a book, and we become the same for that person. As you read the books in the three-year program, think of it as an interpersonal project in which the members of the body of Christ are bonded as brothers and sisters in spiritual growth and Christian understanding.

Step 5: Join a Group

Anyone who has ever been part of a reading group knows the value of discussing ideas among friends who love you but will also challenge you. When we join a group, a natural synergism takes place. The working principle is given to us by Jesus when he says, "Where two or three come together in my name, there I am with them" (Matt. 18:20). Imagine coming together in a reading group with a Christian book as the common subject. The promise is that Christ, through his Holy Spirit, will also become a member, stimulating thought, provoking questions, and leading to conclusions.

Step 6: Own a Thought

As you read a book from the list, look for thoughts that you can embrace as your own. This is not cheating or plagiarism. Every author I know is flattered when a reader grasps a thought that helps him or her better understand the Christian faith. These thoughts become anchors in our walk with God. They steady us, help us define our Christian character, and serve as vehicles for communicating our faith to others. Elton Trueblood's conclusion to his book *The New Man for Our Time* comes to mind. He writes, "It is the vocation of Christians in every generation to outthink all opposition."[1] During the formative years of my faith, when I was also doing graduate study, I wrestled with the role of intellect in my ministry. Trueblood resolved my struggle with these words. I saw that intellectual integrity was not only essential to my faith but that I had an obligation to my generation to "outthink all opposition." In hundreds of speeches and hours of counseling with students, I have used these words again and again. The credit belongs to Trueblood, but his thought is also mine.

Step 7: Pray It Through

Once you have grasped an author's thought and made it your own, it is time to submit the idea in prayer before God in advance of racing down the road to announce and apply it. Too many immature thoughts are passed on because we skip the ripening process of reflective prayer and thoughtful decision making. As a person who has lived through the past fifty years of evangelical Christian history and has known personally most of the leaders of this era, I can assure you that they are as fallible as they are great. In one way or another, I have seen the feet of clay on each of them. Never have I heard one of these Christian leaders deliberately deceive people, but under the press of the moment or seduction of the second, they spoke with later regret. Even the ideas of our most trusted Christian leaders, therefore, need to be tested in the crucible of prayer as well as in the arena of public debate. Prayerful reflection is the best antidote known for a rush to judgment. So before owning an idea that you would be ready to defend, weigh its truth against God's full revelation and embrace it with humility not arrogance.

Step 8: Teach It to Others

A wise and witty man once said, "How do I know what I think until I see what I write?" He reminds us that there is a vast difference between the ideas we frame in our heads and those we put on paper. Writing puts our thoughts at arm's length and forces us to view them objectively. Teaching does the same thing. It is one thing to nurture a thought within ourselves and quite another to say it out loud to others. Therefore, if you want to know what you really think about an idea found in a book, try to explain it to others. Both your knowledge of the idea and your ownership of it will be tested.

The ultimate test of our knowledge is to teach a child. Parents, in particular, have a greater teaching opportunity than any of the world's most renowned scholars. Yet, we remember that the brightest of scholars have also been the greatest teachers. They can take a complex subject and explain it even to a child.

I repeat my favorite story as an example. When I was a very young college president, I found a colleague, friend, and brother in Rev. William MacCleister, senior pastor of the First Presbyterian Church in Jackson, Michigan. Bill, as I knew him, told me about living in Princeton, New Jersey, while attending Princeton Theological Seminary. To help him through his graduate study, his wife taught second grade in the public schools. One day she came home with the story of a second grader who seemed to have a block against learning math. Try as she might with individual attention and special tutoring, the child still failed. But then, to her shock, the boy arrived at school one morning with his math homework completed and all the answers correct. Assuming that someone had done the work for him, Mrs. MacCleister quizzed him on his understanding of the problems and their solutions. Her shock level increased when the boy confidently explained the process and showed how he got his answers. She could only contend, "Someone must have helped you with your math!" "Yes," the boy said, "it was the man across the street." Mrs. MacCleister gasped in total disbelief because she knew that the man across the street was none other than Albert Einstein!

If you want to test your knowledge of your reading, teach a child. Meals around the family dining table can be turned into lively conversations, and family devotions can become times of sharing insights into the Word of God from our reading and study. If the list in this book fulfills its purpose, parents and children will teach and learn from each other in the setting of the Christian home.

Step 9: Search Out a Subject

An additional way to learn a truth is to search out a subject that can be traced throughout the books in this list. Such a practice is called cross-referencing. Assume, for instance, that you are going to teach a lesson on the subject of grace. Reading what different authors have to say about the subject will widen and deepen your understanding.

In the three-year reading plan, for instance, the selections for Bible study include *Understanding the Bible* by John Stott, *What the Bible Is All About* by Henrietta Mears, and *How to Read the Bible for All Its Worth* by Gordon Fee and Douglas Stuart. Although the subject of each book is the same, each of the authors brings a different and enriching viewpoint to the study. In these books, you can also find bibliographies that will point you to other valuable sources that will enrich your understanding of the Word.

Internet connections are fast becoming a ready reference for checking out a variety of books on a given subject. By simply typing in the key word of the subject on a bookstore web site, you can find scores of entries for other books on the same subject. Recently, for example, I wanted to do some research on the subject of grace. My interest in the subject had been piqued by reading Chuck Swindoll's moving account of King David's gracious treatment of Mephibosheth, the crippled grandson of Saul, in his book *The Grace Awakening*. Swindoll uses one sentence in Scripture to summarize the meaning of grace. Although David had the kingly prerogative to wreak vengeance on Saul's family, instead we read four times in 2 Samuel 9 that David said Mephibosheth shall eat at the king's table (2 Sam. 9:7, 10, 11, 13). With a new sense of the meaning of grace, I began my search for other sources. By typing in the word, I found over three thousand entries under the subject. I narrowed down the list and chose a few books for further reading. For starters, I reread Philip Yancey's *What's So Amazing about Grace?* in which he describes the term as the "last best" theological word that has never been spoiled. I then added a touch of meaning from David Seamand's book *Healing Grace*, and then read Paul Tournier's *Guilt and Grace*. Anyone who has experienced the exhilarating moment when the larger meaning of God's revelation bursts into view will follow the path of searching out a subject time and time again.

Step 10: Expand Your Reading

The limits of space did not permit us to include all the exceptional books that qualify for the list. Yet, as you search out subjects through cross-referencing with various authors, you will find other books to read. And as your library grows, you will want to include many of them in your personal collection. To show the range of books that are available to Christian readers in all twelve subject areas, a more complete list of the books recommended by the selection committee is included in appendix A.

Believe it or not, after you have experienced the joys and rewards of reading the books in the three-year plan, you will realize your adventure has just begun. In the world of Christian books, there are untold treasures yet to be mined. We call these treasures "Christian classics" because they offer eternal truth that has stood the test of time. When all is said and done, they qualify as the best words on the Holy Word.

7. Anticipating
the Christian Classics

Age should speak; advanced years should teach wisdom.

Job 32:7

O ne of the hopeful signs for the twenty-first century is the revival of interest in Christian classics. Our generation is known for its self-interest, love of novelty, and drive for relevance. Most of the literature of the day, even Christian literature, seems to reinforce the secular viewpoint. The new generation of Christians, in particular, shows little interest in the long journey of the church through the ages since the time of Jesus Christ. Yet, during these centuries, biblical truth has been defended, faith has been shaped, lives have been changed, and worlds have been won. For this reason, we included Bruce Shelley's *Church History in Plain Language* and Mark Noll's *Turning Points* in the three-year reading plan. Noll's book, in particular, identifies twelve turning points in Christian history that have directly influenced the integrity of our faith through the ages. Christian classics tell that same story through the thoughts, words, and experiences of great saints and great movements. They are not only *worthy* of our reading, they are *essential* to our reading.

A New Interest in Christian Classics

People are showing a renewed interest in Christian classics, possibly because they fear secular society has reached a dead end in moral corruption, social violence, and emotional malaise. William Bennett's *The Book of Virtues* struck a chord with the public mind and with beleaguered parents especially, containing passages of great literature that teach moral values. Stuart and Jill Briscoe addressed the same need from an explicitly Christian viewpoint with their collection of teachable truths called *The Family Book of Christian Values.*

Others have followed with a variety of viewpoints on the Christian classics. One of the most interesting and valuable is the work by Vigen Guroian, *Tending the Heart of Virtue: How Classic Stories Awaken a Child's Moral Imagination.* For those of us who envision Christian classics as long tomes of outdated language and complex thoughts, we will be pleasantly surprised to learn that Guroian finds the same themes of "universally binding morals" in fairy tales and fantasies. *Pinocchio, The Snow Queen, Beauty and the Beast,* The Chronicles of Narnia series, *The Little Mermaid, The Velveteen Rabbit,* and *The*

Prince and the Goblin all qualify as classics that support the Christian faith, according to the author. Why? Because they contend for moral absolutes in the contest between good and evil, cultivate the moral imagination, and develop moral discernment. Perhaps to our surprise, Guroian found that fourth graders understand and accept these truths more than college students. If we can cultivate these gifts of understanding and acceptance among our children, they will be ready readers of Christian classics in the future.

What Is a Christian Classic?

Definitions of Christian classics range all the way from homespun humor to heady scholarship. Mark Twain, the master humorist, described a classic as "a book that people praise and don't read." Elton Trueblood gave the definition a more serious bent: "It is a book that has been tested." C. S. Lewis added the dimension of time to the test when he wrote, "The only palliative (for the mistakes of our time) is to keep the clean sea breeze of the centuries blowing through our minds, and this can be done only by reading old books. Not, of course, that there is any magic about the past. People were no cleverer than they are now; they made the same many mistakes as we. But not the same mistakes." Lewis then reinforced this idea by offering this principle: "It is a good rule, after reading a new book, never to allow yourself another new one 'til you have read an old one in between."[1]

The test of time, however, does not necessarily confirm the quality of the content. Robert Maynard Hutchins, editor in chief for the *Great Books of the Western World*, describes great books as those "that had endured and the common voice of mankind called the finest creation, in writing, of the Western mind."[2] For him, books that meet these qualifications will contribute to what he calls "The Great Conversation" between students and scholars, which, in turn, leads to a "liberal education."

Still, the tests of time and creativity do not provide an assurance of quality. As we now know, liberal education in many colleges and universities means politically correct choices in reading, which means the writings of dead, white, Western, and Christian males are taboo. This bias is corrected by Louise Cowan, coeditor with Os Guinness of the book *Invitation to the Classics*. She answers the question, "What is a classic?" by listing seven characteristics:

1. The classics not only exhibit distinguished style, fine artistry, and keen intellect but create whole universes of imagination and thought.
2. They portray life as complex and many-sided, depicting both negative and positive aspects of human character in the process of discovering and testing enduring virtues.
3. They have a transforming effect on the reader's self-understanding.
4. They invite and survive frequent rereadings.
5. They adapt themselves to various times and places and provide a sense of the shared life of humanity.
6. They are considered classics by a sufficiently large number of people, establishing themselves with common readers as well as qualified authorities.
7. Finally, their appeal endures over wide reaches of time.[3]

The working definition we used to choose books for the three-year reading plan is consistent with these criteria. To distinguish a distinctly Christian classic, however, we added to the requirement of literary quality the standards of biblical integrity, lay readability, and developmental value for Christian understanding and spiritual growth. Admittedly, the books we chose have not yet passed the test of time, and whether they will survive the test of time is yet unknown.

Historians have a rule of thumb that it takes at least seventy-five years before we can gain perspective on a contemporary event. The same might be said for books. It will take at least seventy-five years for the books published in our generation to be retained as classics or discarded among millions of forgettable titles. Ultimately, the test of timeless truth will determine their destiny.

Christian Classic Collections

The revival of interest in Christian classics has been led by several prominent Christian writers who have compiled lists of books for consideration.

Devotional Classics

Perhaps best known is Eugene Peterson, author of the Message, who has also written a book entitled *Take and Read* in which he selects a wide variety of works emphasizing spirituality and gives a brief description of each book. Among the books chosen as classics, or as he puts it, "the giants in the land," are the more familiar Thomas à Kempis's *Imitation of Christ*, Blaise Pascal's *Pensees*, John Bunyan's *Pilgrim's Progress*, and Søren Kierkegaard's *Purity of Heart Is to Will One Thing*. Peterson's list is highly personal, but when an author of his stature makes his recommendations for spiritual classics, people take note.

The devotional life has become a major interest among believers of late, prompting many to read books on the subject of spirituality. My close friend and colleague Donald Demaray, Senior Beeson Professor of Preaching at Asbury Theological Seminary, teaches courses on the devotional life in which he involves his students in both the study and practice of spiritual disciplines. His reading list of devotional classics is "classic" in itself. Demaray introduces us to the lives and writings of such ancients as John Chrysostom and Catherine of Siena as well as our twentieth-century contemporaries Thomas Merton and Elizabeth O'Connor.

I asked Dr. Demaray to choose twenty of those devotional classics as recommended reading for Christian laity. Although he struggled to limit the number to twenty, Dr. Demaray took the challenge and gave us the list found in appendix B. For those who are especially interested in devotional literature and spirituality, Demaray's list is an invitation to a lifetime of solid reading in the classics.

Classics on Jesus

Calvin Miller, one of Christianity's most creative speakers and writers, has also compiled a collection of classical writing called *The Book of Jesus: A Treasury of the Greatest Stories and Writings about Christ*. Books, stories, poems, and hymns take us through the centuries and through the life of Christ. In the books he has chosen, Miller ranges from Christian fathers such as St. Athanasius and St. Francis to contemporary writers such as Charles Colson and Max Lucado. He also adds some surprises with insights into the life of Christ from Shakespeare, Mahatma Gandhi, Desmond Tutu, and even Ernest Hemingway. Both his choice of writings and his divisions of the life of Jesus are intriguing:

Jesus: Who He Was
Jesus: His Birth
Jesus: His Friendship with Us All
Jesus: His Becoming One of Us
Jesus: His Miracles
Jesus: His Teachings
Jesus: His Cross

Jesus: His Resurrection
Jesus: His Continuing Reign
Jesus: His Second Coming

As always, Miller never fails to stimulate our mind and spirit as he puts a creative touch to his solid faith in each of these sections. The book serves as a ready source of inspiration when we have just a minute or two to read a short selection from a great author.

Classics in the Christian Tradition

Terry Glaspey takes on the larger task of identifying *Great Books of the Christian Tradition* from the time of the ancient world to the present day. In response to his own question, "Why read the Christian classics?" he gives six answers: (1) appreciating our diversity; (2) appreciating the depth of our heritage; (3) asking the perennial questions; (4) seeing beyond today; (5) building a Christian vision; and (6) learning from the past. Chronologically, then, Glaspey chooses Christian classics from the ancient world, the early modern world, the eighteenth century, the nineteenth century, the twentieth century, and he even dares to recommend contemporary books as "candidates for greatness." His most daring decision, however, is to list ten books that are classics among the classics. They are:

1. *The Confessions*, St. Augustine
2. *The Divine Comedy*, Dante
3. *The Imitation of Christ*, Thomas à Kempis
4. *The Practice of the Presence of God*, Brother Lawrence
5. *Pensees*, Blaise Pascal
6. *The Pilgrim's Progress*, John Bunyan
7. *The Brothers Karamazov*, Fyodor Dostoyevsky
8. *The Pursuit of God*, A. W. Tozer

9. *Mere Christianity*, C. S. Lewis
10. *Celebration of Discipline*, Richard Foster

Secular Classics with Christian Insights

The most complete and far-ranging work on classics with Christian insights is *Invitation to the Classics*, edited by Louise Cowan and Os Guinness. The editors and their team of scholars take on the arduous task of reviewing great writings, beginning with Homer's *Iliad* and *Odyssey* and journeying through the centuries to contemporary writers such as Aleksandr Solzhenitsyn. In each case, one of the contributing editors writes a synopsis of the book and focuses on a universal truth that is consistent with a Christian worldview.

Critics will be quick to find fault with their approach. In a day when we get news by sound bites, read condensed versions of best-selling books, and rely on synopses of stories to bring us up to date, we are tempted to substitute reading about the classics for reading the classics themselves. Another question may be raised about the character of the authors, such as William Shakespeare, whose drama can soar into the heights of spiritual truth and then plummet into the depths of ribald humor. Nevertheless, *Invitation to the Classics* is a monumental work that deserves a place on our reading shelf. Also, its value as a reference source prompts us to include its list of classics as a guide for future reading (see appendix C).

If you want the rich experience of sitting at the feet of a great Christian teacher of classical literature, you must read *Realms of Gold: The Classics in Christian Perspective* by Leland Ryken. Although Ryken, professor of English at Wheaton College, is a distinguished scholar in his field, he has the rare ability to make the classics come alive for lay readers. As you read the book, you will sense that you are sitting in his classroom, learning to love great literature, gaining an understanding of its value, and especially seeing how the classics contribute to a Christian perspective of life. With the touch of a great teacher, Ryken brings simplicity to a complex subject by clearly outlining his thoughts and succinctly summarizing his conclusions. Consequently, you will come away from the book with an appetite whetted to read the books that once seemed too formidable: Homer's *Odyssey*, Chaucer's *Canterbury Tales*, Shakespeare's *Macbeth*, Milton's *Paradise Lost*, Hawthorne's *Scarlet Letter*, Dickens's *Great Expectations*, Tolstoy's *The Death of Ivan Ilych*, and Camus's *The Stranger*.

Ryken sees the rewards that come with all great literature: "pleasure, recreation, heightened awareness of human experience, involvement with life, expanded viewpoint, and the occasion to focus our own thinking about the great issues of life."[4] More than that, Ryken says that reading the classics has two special benefits for the contemporary Christian reader.

> First, we can expect our reading of the classics to make us discontent with shallow forms of literature, including examples from television drama and movies. As our taste is trained by contact with excellence, lesser works will inevitably seem inferior. Secondly, contact with the classics will alert us to the literary excellence of the Bible. The Bible, too, is a literary classic. It possesses the literary beauty, power, and wisdom that the best literature possesses. It is more than a literary classic, but not less.[5]

Religious Books of the Twentieth Century

Since the time of its founding more than fifty years ago, *Christianity Today* has surveyed its readership to publish a list of the most important Christian books of the year. In the April 24, 2000, issue of the magazine, the editors listed their choices for the one hundred books of the century that were already identified as classics. Out of this list, the editors asked scholars and church leaders to select the ten best religious books of the twentieth century. Criteria for selection included importance at the time of publishing and enduring significance for the Christian faith and the church. Even books with which evangelical Christians might not agree are included because we must contend with their influence on our faith and practice. The following books were chosen as the ten best religious books of the twentieth century.

1. *Mere Christianity*, C. S. Lewis
2. *The Cost of Discipleship*, Dietrich Bonhoeffer
3. *Church Dogmatics*, Karl Barth
4. *The Lord of the Rings* (trilogy), J. R. R. Tolkien
5. *The Politics of Jesus*, John Yoder
6. *Orthodoxy*, G. K. Chesterton
7. *The Seven Storey Mountain*, Thomas Merton
8. *Celebration of Discipline*, Richard Foster
9. *My Utmost for His Highest*, Oswald Chambers
10. *Moral Man and Immoral Society*, Reinhold Niebuhr

With few exceptions, each of these books can be read by Christian laypersons. Several were also included in the three-year reading plan contained in this book. As an incentive to further reading of quality Christian books, appendix D contains the full list of *Christianity Today's* one hundred books of the century.

Selected Classics of the Twentieth Century

As a complement to the search for Christian classics, secular publishers have also asked, "What are the most significant books written in the twentieth century?" By surveying authors and editors, they too came up with a list of one hundred books that define the past one hundred years. Sadly, few of them are religious and fewer still were chosen for their spiritual insights. A quick review of the top ten choices reveals why President Bill Clinton, a Rhodes scholar and avid reader, confessed after reading the list, "I feel as if I am ignorant." Most of us may feel the same way when we see the list.

Nonfiction
1. *The Education of Henry Adams*, Henry Adams
2. *The Varieties of Religious Experience*, William James
3. *Up from Slavery*, Booker T. Washington
4. *A Room of One's Own*, Virginia Woolf
5. *Silent Spring*, Rachel Carson
6. *Selected Essays, 1917–1932*, T. S. Eliot
7. *The Double Helix*, James D. Watson
8. *Speak, Memory*, Vladimir Nabokov
9. *The American Language*, H. L. Mencken
10. *The General Theory of Employment, Interest, and Money*, John Maynard Keynes

Fiction
1. *Ulysses*, James Joyce
2. *The Great Gatsby*, F. Scott Fitzgerald
3. *A Portrait of the Artist as a Young Man*, James Joyce
4. *Lolita*, Vladimir Nabokov
5. *Brave New World*, Aldous Huxley
6. *The Sound and the Fury*, William Faulkner
7. *Catch-22*, Joseph Heller
8. *Darkness at Noon*, Arthur Koestler
9. *Sons and Lovers*, D. H. Lawrence
10. *The Grapes of Wrath*, John Steinbeck

Regretfully, none of the top one hundred books of the twentieth century is a work published by a Christian press. In fact, none of the books has a specific religious focus except for William James's psychological study *The Varieties of Religious Experience*. And yet, every one of the top ten choices for nonfiction and fiction in the twentieth century reflects a worldview that cannot be ignored, whether Christian or secular. Quite naturally, then, we must ask, "Should Christians read secular books?" The answer is a selective yes. Secular books, and particularly those that are highly recommended by critical review, give added depth and breadth to the perspective of the Christian mind. Like the sharpening of iron against iron, they will challenge and confirm our Christian worldview. They will also teach us to be discerning readers because secular books cannot be read uncritically.

Beth McDonald, one of the professors whom I hired to teach literature at Spring Arbor College (Michigan), was very circumspect in her Christian life. With all due caution, she avoided any appearance of evil. But when it came to teaching English and American literature as a core discipline in the Christian liberal arts, she approached literary works with questionable language or scenes by reminding her students, "We can't stop the birds from flying over our heads, but we can stop them from building nests." In other words, to be liberally educated Christians, the students needed to read secular literature, but they did not have to absorb the values or espouse the viewpoints.

In the book *Invitation to the Classics,* we see another reason for reading secular literature. Too often, believers give up early on books that are not transparently Christian or filled with evangelical jargon. Cowan and Guinness have done us a special service by probing the surface of images, languages, and plots to discover truths that are rooted in biblical Christianity and contain the potential for redemptive hope.

Recently, I finished reading John Grisham's best-seller *The Testament.* As I read, I found my faith resonating with Grisham's story of the wastrel attorney who discovers the beauty and meaning of a Christian missionary who lives selflessly for primitive Indian tribes in the remote Brazilian jungle. She proves her faith by refusing to claim the inheritance that would have made her one of the world's richest women. Not only does the testimony of her life bring the attorney to faith, but between every line in Grisham's story is the repudiation of the false values that are driving us in our secular society. An author's faith is not so evident in most contemporary novels, but Grisham's work reminds us that God can reveal his truth in many ways.

Still another reason for selectively reading secular literature is to be alert to what the world is thinking and feeling. A periodic check of the *New York Times* best-seller index can be most enlightening. Not long ago, the index showed a surprising number of best-sellers that dealt with the subject of spirituality. Even though they ranged from *Chicken Soup for the Soul* to Thomas Merton's *The Seven Storey Mountain*, the signal was clear: Deep within the human psyche of this generation, there is a thirst to know God. Books on Eastern religion, personalistic psychology, the cult of self-realization, and New Age philosophy give us a base for understanding contemporary beliefs and help us find an entry point for Christian witness.

Christian Classics: Old and New

As a fitting conclusion to the many recommendations of books that might qualify as Christian classics, we can return to the challenge, "Imagine that you are to be exiled all alone on a deserted island. You are given the privilege of taking your Bible and ten books with you. Which ten books would you choose?"

The task is even more difficult now because our choices will include old books already acknowledged as Christian classics and new books that are yet to pass the test of time. Yet, as we remember from the pyramid principle, only a handful of books can be read more than once and will grow with us. With this thought in mind, I made a list for my library in exile. Originally, my list included more than fifty books, old and new, fact and fiction, prose and poetry. Finally, after making many difficult choices, I came to my list of ten. The books that I would want to read again and again are the following:

1. *The Confessions,* St. Augustine
   Without question, *The Confessions* is the autobiography of autobiographies. In his search for God, Augustine gives us intellectual and spiritual insights in a context of prayer and praise that have never been matched.
2. *The Imitation of Christ,* Thomas à Kempis
   Here is the prototype for all devotional literature. The author awakens in us a thirst for the purity of spirit and simplicity of life that comes only as we wholeheartedly adore Christ and seek to follow him.
3. *Pensees,* Blaise Pascal
   When Pascal writes, "The heart has reasons of which reason knows nothing," he frames the paradox out of which profound thoughts and great truths are born.
4. *The Brothers Karamazov,* Fyodor Dostoyevsky
   If I had only one novel to read, *The Brothers Karamazov* would be my choice. Dostoyevsky probes the depth of human sin and the height of Christ's redemptive power.
5. *The Pursuit of God/The Knowledge of the Holy,* A. W. Tozer
   By counting these two small books as one, we would encounter the mind and spirit of a man with a deep and abiding sense of the presence of God.
6. *The Four Quartets,* T. S. Eliot
   Poetry with rhythm and depth is a life-support system for a desert island. Form, line, and color all come together in this artistic masterpiece.
7. *The Screwtape Letters,* C. S. Lewis
   Satan cannot stand ridicule and a person exiled on a desert island cannot lose a sense of humor. Lewis's ability to convey truth in satire will dispel loneliness with a laugh.

8. *The Cross of Christ,* John Stott

   If contemporary Christianity is to survive, the doctrine of the cross must be its lifeline. As always, John Stott speaks the truth with love.

9. *In the Name of Jesus,* Henri J. M. Nouwen

   With penetrating spiritual insights, Nouwen identifies the three temptations of leaders, whether in isolation or among the masses. Who can ever forget God's call to Nouwen, "Go among the poor in spirit, and I will heal you"?

10. *The Incendiary Fellowship,* Elton Trueblood

    As a cure for the tendency toward introspection that comes with isolation, Trueblood will not let us forget that we are members of the body of Christ with a fiery passion for the salvation of the world.

We are now ready for exile. With our Bible in hand and ten books in our briefcase, we have an intellectual and spiritual survival kit for use on a lonely island. More than survival is at stake. During our exile, we must grow intellectually and spiritually by reading and rereading the books we have chosen.

What books would make up your library in exile? What classic Christian books do you want to read and reread? As you begin to read books that will lead to your own Christian understanding and spiritual growth, you will make discoveries that you can claim as your own. Like an explorer mapping the way over uncharted territory, you will find classic books that serve as landmarks showing the way and contemporary books that serve as locators defining reality. The text is not dead. Whatever the medium for the books of the future, we must remember that "in the beginning was the Word," which shall never pass away. God's Word and the books that are commentaries on his Word will still be communicators of the faith "once delivered to the saints."

Notes

Chapter 1: Why Christians Are Readers

1. Mortimer Adler and Charles Van Doren, *How to Read a Book* (New York: Simon and Schuster, 1972), 293–95.

2. Ibid., 294–95.

Chapter 4: Reading Christian Books as a Spiritual Discipline

1. Adler and Van Doren, *How to Read a Book*, 4–6.

2. Ibid., 46–47.

3. Ibid., 163–67.

4. Ibid., 309–36.

Chapter 5: Planning a Personal Christian Library

1. Ibid., 341.

2. Ibid., 392.

3. Ibid., 343.

Chapter 6: Introducing a Three-Year Christian Reading Plan

1. Elton Trueblood, *The New Man for Our Time* (New York: Harper & Row, 1970), 126.

Chapter 7: Anticipating the Christian Classics

1. C. S. Lewis, quoted in *Invitation to the Classics*, Louise Cowan and Os Guinness, eds. (Grand Rapids: Baker, 1998), 18.

2. Robert Maynard Hutchins, *The Great Conversation* (Chicago: Encyclopedia Britannica, 1952), xi.

3. *Invitation to the Classics*, 21–22.

4. Leland Ryken, *Realms of Gold: The Classics in Christian Perspective* (Wheaton: Harold Shaw, 1991), 226–27.

5. Ibid., 223.

Appendix A Reference Library for Christian Readers

Following is the list of books the selection committee considered for the three-year reading plan. The thirty-six volumes that eventually made the list are in bold. Those that follow in each category received fewer votes from the selection committee, but they are also recommended, without hesitation, for your reading.

Autobiography/Biography

Through Gates of Splendor, **Elisabeth Elliot**
Just as I Am, **Billy Graham**
Surprised by Joy, **C. S. Lewis**
Here I Stand, **Roland Bainton**
The Hiding Place, Corrie ten Boom
Born Again, Charles Colson
A Song of Ascents, E. Stanley Jones
Shadow of the Almighty, Elisabeth Elliot

Church History

Church History in Plain Language, **Bruce Shelley**
Turning Points, **Mark Noll**

Revivalism and Social Reform, Timothy Smith

Christianity through the Ages, Kenneth Latourette

Discovering an Evangelical Heritage, Donald Dayton

The Democratization of American Christianity, Nathan Hatch

Evangelicalism and the Future of Christianity, Alister McGrath

In Search of Christian America, Mark Noll, Nathan Hatch, and George Marsden

Evangelical Renaissance, Donald Bloesch

Christianity through the Centuries, Earle Cairns

Bible Study

Understanding the Bible, John Stott

What the Bible Is All About, Henrietta Mears

How to Read the Bible for All Its Worth, Gordon Fee and Douglas Stuart

The Message of the New Testament, F. F. Bruce

A Theology of the New Testament, George Ladd

Old Testament Introduction, William Lasor, David Hubbard, and Frederic Bush

Twelve Dynamic Bible Study Methods, Rick Warren

Methodical Bible Study, Robert Traina

Worship

Worship His Majesty, Jack Hayford

Real Worship, Warren Wiersbe

Worship Is a Verb, Robert Webber

Reaching Out without Dumbing Down, Marva Dawn

Devotion and Prayer

My Utmost for His Highest, Oswald Chambers

Power through Prayer, E. M. Bounds

A Diary of Private Prayer, John Baillie

The Practice of the Presence of God, Brother Lawrence

Practicing His Presence, Frank Laubach and Brother Lawrence

With Christ in the School of Prayer, Andrew Murray

The Way, E. Stanley Jones
Prayer: Finding the Heart's True Home, Richard Foster

Spiritual Discipline

Celebration of Discipline, **Richard Foster**
The Spirit of the Disciplines, **Dallas Willard**
The Cost of Discipleship, **Dietrich Bonhoeffer**
The Pursuit of God, A. W. Tozer
A Long Obedience in the Same Direction, Eugene Peterson
Radical Commitment, Vernon Grounds
The Path to Perfection, W. E. Sangster
The Taste of New Wine, Keith Miller
Journey Inward, Journey Outward, Elizabeth O'Connor

Theology

The Jesus I Never Knew, **Philip Yancey**
Knowing God, **J. I. Packer**
Mere Christianity, **C. S. Lewis**
Basic Christianity, John Stott
The Knowledge of the Holy, A. W. Tozer
Your God Is Too Small, J. B. Phillips
The Cross of Christ, John Stott
The Divine Conspiracy, Dallas Willard
How to Be Born Again, Billy Graham
The Gospel in a Pluralist Society, Lesslie Newbigen

The Church

The Body, **Charles Colson**
The Company of the Committed, **Elton Trueblood**
The Incendiary Fellowship, Elton Trueblood
The Purpose-Driven Church, Rick Warren
A Church for the Twenty-first Century, Leith Anderson
The Community of the King, Howard Snyder

Evangelism and Missions

How to Give Away Your Faith, **Paul Little**
The Master Plan of Evangelism, **Robert Coleman**
Out of the Salt Shaker and into the World, **Rebecca Manley Pippert**
Christian Mission in the Modern World, John Stott
How to Reach Secular People, George Hunter
Lifestyle Evangelism, Joe Aldrich
Evangelism Explosion, James Kennedy
Becoming a Contagious Christian, Bill Hybels and Mark Mittelberg

The Family

Children

How to Lead Your Child to Christ, **Luis and Pat Palau**
Letters to Karen, Charlie Shedd
Promises to Peter, Charlie Shedd
Joining Children on the Spiritual Journey, Catherine Stonehouse

Youth

You Can Make a Difference, Tony Campolo
Parents and Teenagers, Jay Kesler, editor

Marriage

I Married You, **Walter Trobisch**
Sex for Christians, Lewis Smedes
Making Love Last Forever, Gary Smalley
The Committed Marriage, Elizabeth Achtemeier
Love Must Be Tough, James Dobson

Parenting

Dare to Discipline, **James Dobson**
The Family Book of Christian Values, Stuart and Jill Briscoe

Christian Living

Healing for Damaged Emotions, **David Seamands**

Reference Library for Christian Readers

127

Forgive and Forget, **Lewis Smedes**
The Meaning of Persons, **Paul Tournier**
The Four Loves, C. S. Lewis
Loving God, Charles Colson
Discovering God's Will in Your Life, Lloyd Ogilvie
Ordering Your Private World, Gordon MacDonald
Where Is God When It Hurts? Philip Yancey

Christian Social Action

Let Justice Roll Down, **John Perkins**
Rich Christians in an Age of Hunger, **Ronald Sider**
The Politics of Jesus, **John Yoder**
The Social Conscience of the Evangelical, Sherwood Wirt
Uncommon Decency, Richard Mouw
The Mark of the Christian, Francis Schaeffer
Money, Sex and Power, Richard Foster
Resident Aliens, Stanley Hauerwas and William Willimon
Black and Free, Tom Skinner
The Mustard Seed Conspiracy, Tom Sine

Apologetics and Ethics

The Christian Mind, **Harry Blamires**
God in the Dock, C. S. Lewis
The God Who Is There, Francis Schaeffer
Your Mind Matters, John Stott
Letters from a Skeptic, Greg Boyd
A Place to Stand, Elton Trueblood
Mere Morality, Lewis Smedes
The Scandal of the Evangelical Mind, Mark Noll

Appendix A

Appendix B Great Books
of Christian Devotion

Following are devotional classics recommended for lay readers by Dr. Donald Demaray, Senior Beeson Professor of Homiletics at Asbury Theological Seminary and teacher of a course in which he and his students read these classics and join together in devotions.

The Confessions, St. Augustine

A Diary of Private Prayer, John Baillie

The Cost of Discipleship, Dietrich Bonhoeffer

The Sacrament of the Present Moment, Jean-Pierre De Caussade

Prayer: Finding the Heart's True Home, Richard Foster

Experiencing the Depths of Jesus Christ, Jeanne Guyon

The Spiritual Exercises of St. Ignatius, Ignatius of Loyola

Abundant Living, E. Stanley Jones

Showings, Julian of Norwich

The Imitation of Christ, Thomas à Kempis

Famous Conversions, Hugh T. Kerr and John M. Mulder, editors

A Serious Call to a Devout and Holy Life, William Law

The Practice of the Presence of God, Brother Lawrence
Deeper Experiences of Famous Christians, J. Gilchrist Lawson, editor
Practicing His Presence, Frank Laubach and Brother Lawrence
The Seven Storey Mountain, Thomas Merton
The Wounded Healer, Henri J. M. Nouwen
Pensees, Blaise Pascal
The Christian's Secret of a Happy Life, Hannah Whitall Smith
The Daily Wesley, John Wesley

Appendix C Accepting an Invitation to the Classics

Following is a list of great works cited in *Invitation to the Classics*, edited by Louise Cowan and Os Guinness. The book is particularly helpful to lay readers because each of the classics is introduced by information about the author, a brief summary of its content, and a statement regarding its contribution to a Christian perspective.

The Iliad; and *Odyssey,* Homer
The Oresteia, Aeschylus
History of the Persian Wars, Herodotus
Oedipus Rex, Sophocles
The Bacchae, Euripides
Comedies, Aristophanes
The Republic, Plato
Nichomachean Ethics, Aristotle
The Aeneid, Virgil
The Confessions, St. Augustine
Beowulf
Summa Theologica, Thomas Aquinas

The Divine Comedy, Dante

The Canterbury Tales, Geoffrey Chaucer

The Second Shepherds' Play; and *Everyman*

Utopia, Thomas More

The Babylonian Captivity of the Church; and *The Small Catechism,* Martin Luther

The Prince, Niccolò Machiavelli

Institutes of the Christian Religion, John Calvin

Don Quixote, Miguel de Cervantes

Hamlet; King Lear; Midsummer Night's Dream; and *The Tempest,* William Shakespeare

Poems, John Donne

The Temple, George Herbert

Paradise Lost, John Milton

Pensees, Blaise Pascal

The Pilgrim's Progress, John Bunyan

Gulliver's Travels, Jonathan Swift

A Treatise Concerning Religious Affections, Jonathan Edwards

Essays; and *Rasselas,* Samuel Johnson

The Life of Samuel Johnson, LL.D., James Boswell

Confessions, Jean-Jacques Rousseau

The Federalist, Alexander Hamilton, James Madison, and John Jay

Pride and Prejudice, Jane Austen

Faust, Johann Wolfgang von Goethe

Lyrical Ballads, Williams Wordsworth and Samuel Taylor Coleridge

The Great Odes, John Keats

Democracy in America, Alexis de Tocqueville

Essays, Ralph Waldo Emerson

Narrative of the Life of Frederick Douglass, Frederick Douglass

The Scarlet Letter, Nathaniel Hawthorne

The Complete Poems, Emily Dickinson

Moby Dick, Herman Melville

Madame Bovary, Gustave Flaubert

Great Expectations, Charles Dickens

Apologia pro vita sua, John Henry, Cardinal Newman

Fear and Trembling, Søren Kierkegaard

Middlemarch, George Eliot
Poems, Gerard Manley Hopkins
Anna Karenina, Leo Tolstoy
The Brothers Karamazov, Fyodor Dostoyevsky
The Portrait of a Lady, Henry James
The Adventures of Huckleberry Finn, Mark Twain
Twilight of the Idols, Friedrich Nietzsche
Heart of Darkness, Joseph Conrad
Dubliners, James Joyce
The Trial, Franz Kafka
Poems, William Butler Yeats
Four Quartets, T. S. Eliot
Poems, Robert Frost
The Screwtape Letters, C. S. Lewis
Go Down, Moses, William Faulkner
Waiting for God, Simone Weil
Letters and Papers from Prison, Dietrich Bonhoeffer
"A Good Man Is Hard to Find"; "Greenleaf"; and "Revelation," Flannery O'Connor
One Day in the Life of Ivan Denisovich, Aleksandr Solzhenitsyn

Appendix D *Christianity Today*
Books of the Century

Following is *Christianity Today*'s list of one hundred books chosen by leaders and thinkers as "best" for shaping contemporary religious thought and having "enduring significance for the Christian faith and the church." Only the first ten are listed in order of importance. The other ninety are in alphabetical order by author.

1. *Mere Christianity*, C. S. Lewis
2. *The Cost of Discipleship*, Dietrich Bonhoeffer
3. *Church Dogmatics*, Karl Barth
4. *The Lord of the Rings* (trilogy), J. R. R. Tolkien
5. *The Politics of Jesus*, John Yoder
6. *Orthodoxy*, G. K. Chesterton
7. *The Seven Storey Mountain*, Thomas Merton
8. *Celebration of Discipline*, Richard Foster
9. *My Utmost for His Highest*, Oswald Chambers
10. *Moral Man and Immoral Society*, Reinhold Niebuhr

Things Fall Apart, Chinua Achebe
The Big Book of Alcoholics Anonymous, Alcoholics Anonymous

Here I Stand, Roland Bainton
The Epistle to the Romans, Karl Barth
The Denial of Death, Ernest Becker
Habits of the Heart, Robert N. Bellah et al.
The Diary of the Country Priest, Georges Bernanos
Letters and Papers from Prison, Dietrich Bonhoeffer
Transforming Mission, David Bosch
The Prophetic Imagination, Walter Brueggemann
Truth as Encounter, Emil Brunner
The Plague, Albert Camus
The Case for Orthodox Theology, Edward John Carnell
Death Comes for the Archbishop, Willa Cather
The Long Loneliness, Dorothy Day
Pilgrim at Tinker Creek, Annie Dillard
The Documents of Vatican II
The Souls of Black Folk, W. E. B. Du Bois
Four Quartets, T. S. Eliot
Invisible Man, Ralph Ellison
The Technological Society, Jacques Ellul
Silence, Shusaku Endo
The Diary of Anne Frank, Anne Frank
Man's Search for Meaning, Viktor Frankl
Civilization and Its Discontents, Sigmund Freud
The Fundamentals
Shantung Compound, Langdon Gilkey
In a Different Voice, Carol Gilligan
The Power and the Glory, Graham Greene
Black Like Me, John Howard Griffin
A Theology of Liberation, Gustavo Gutierrez
Lest Innocent Blood Be Shed, Philip Paul Hallie
A Community of Character, Stanley Hauerwas
Living in Truth, Vaclav Havel
The Moral Vision of the New Testament, Richard Hays
God, Revelation, and Authority (six volumes), Carl F. H. Henry
Hiroshima, John R. Hersey
The Prophets, Abraham Heschel

Brave New World, Aldous Huxley

The Varieties of Religious Experience, William James

The Trial, Franz Kafka

A Testament of Hope, Martin Luther King Jr.

The Structure of Scientific Revolutions, Thomas S. Kuhn

To Kill a Mockingbird, Harper Lee

A Sand County Almanac, Aldo Leopold

The Chronicles of Narnia series (especially *The Lion, the Witch, and the Wardrobe*); and *The Screwtape Letters*, C. S. Lewis

Christianity and Liberalism, J. Gresham Machen

After Virtue, Alasdair C. MacIntyre

The Autobiography of Malcolm X, Malcolm X and Alex Haley

Fundamentalism and American Culture, George M. Marsden

Vipers' Tangle, Francois Mauriac

The Crucified God, Jurgen Moltmann

The Naked Public Square, Richard John Neuhaus

The Gospel in a Pluralist Society, Lesslie Newbigin

Christ and Culture, H. Richard Niebuhr

The Nature and Destiny of Man (two volumes), Reinhold Niebuhr

The Cloister Walk, Kathleen Norris

The Wounded Healer, Henri J. M. Nouwen

Agape and Eros, Anders Nygren

Journey Inward, Journey Outward, Elizabeth O'Connor

A Good Man Is Hard to Find, and Other Stories, Flannery O'Connor

The Idea of the Holy, Rudolf Otto

Knowing God, J. I. Packer

Cry, the Beloved Country, Alan Paton

Jesus through the Centuries, Jaroslav Pelikan

The Four Cardinal Virtues, Josef Pieper

Personal Knowledge, Michael Polanyi

The Chosen, Chaim Potok

Christianity and the Social Crisis, Walter Rauschenbusch

The Mind of the Maker, Dorothy L. Sayers

The Quest of the Historical Jesus, Albert Schweitzer

On the Beach, Nevil Shute

Rich Christians in an Age of Hunger, Ronald J. Sider

The Gulag Archipelago; and *One Day in the Life of Ivan Denisovich*, Aleksandr Solzhenitsyn

Basic Christianity, John Stott

The Meaning of Persons, Paul Tournier

The Pursuit of God, A. W. Tozer

The Guns of August, Barbara Tuchman

Mysticism, Evelyn Underhill

Exclusion and Embrace, Miroslav Volf

Old Testament Theology, Gerhard von Rad

The Missionary Movement in Christian History, Andrew F. Walls

The Protestant Ethic and the Spirit of Capitalism, Max Weber

Waiting for God, Simone Weil

Night, Elie Wiesel

Descent into Hell, Charles Williams

Engaging the Powers, Walter Wink

The Jesus I Never Knew, Philip Yancey

Appendix E Books of the Century for the Modern Library

Nonfiction

At the close of the twentieth century, the Modern Library made its selection of the one hundred best nonfiction books published during this century. Religious writings are rare, but the selected books inform Christian readers about the thinking of the contemporary mind, the challenges that are presented to our faith, and the way in which the Holy Spirit still works through the human mind. The books are ranked in order of importance.

1. *The Education of Henry Adams*, Henry Adams
2. *The Varieties of Religious Experience*, William James
3. *Up from Slavery*, Booker T. Washington
4. *A Room of One's Own*, Virginia Woolf
5. *Silent Spring*, Rachel Carson
6. *Selected Essays, 1917–1932*, T. S. Eliot
7. *The Double Helix*, James D. Watson
8. *Speak, Memory*, Vladimir Nabokov
9. *The American Language*, H. L. Mencken

10. *The General Theory of Employment, Interest, and Money,* John Maynard Keynes
11. *The Lives of a Cell,* Lewis Thomas
12. *The Frontier in American History,* Frederick Jackson Turner
13. *Black Boy,* Richard Wright
14. *Aspects of the Novel,* E. M. Forster
15. *The Civil War,* Shelby Foote
16. *The Guns of August,* Barbara Tuchman
17. *The Proper Study of Mankind,* Isaiah Berlin
18. *The Nature and Destiny of Man,* Reinhold Niebuhr
19. *Notes of a Native Son,* James Baldwin
20. *The Autobiography of Alice B. Toklas,* Gertrude Stein
21. *The Elements of Style,* William Strunk and E. B. White
22. *An American Dilemma,* Gunnar Myrdal
23. *Principia Mathematica,* Alfred North Whitehead and Bertrand Russell
24. *The Mismeasure of Man,* Stephen Jay Gould
25. *The Mirror and the Lamp,* Meyer Howard Adams
26. *Pluto's Republic,* Peter B. Medawar
27. *The Ants,* Bert Holldobler and Edward O. Wilson
28. *A Theory of Justice,* John Rawls
29. *Art and Illusion,* Ernest H. Gombrich
30. *The Making of the English Working Class,* E. P. Thompson
31. *The Souls of Black Folk,* W. E. B. Du Bois
32. *Principia Ethica,* G. E. Moore
33. *Philosophy and Civilization,* John Dewey
34. *On Growth and Form,* D'Arcy Thompson
35. *Ideas and Opinions,* Albert Einstein
36. *The Age of Jackson,* Arthur Schlesinger Jr.
37. *The Making of the Atomic Bomb,* Richard Rhodes
38. *Black Lamb and Grey Falcon,* Rebecca West
39. *Autobiographies,* W. B. Yeats
40. *Science and Civilisation in China,* Joseph Needham
41. *Goodbye to All That,* Robert Graves
42. *Homage to Catalonia,* George Orwell
43. *The Autobiography of Mark Twain,* Mark Twain
44. *Children of Crisis,* Robert Coles
45. *A Study of History,* Arnold J. Toynbee
46. *The Affluent Society,* John Kenneth Galbraith
47. *Present at the Creation,* Dean Acheson
48. *The Great Bridge,* David McCullough
49. *Patriotic Gore,* Edmund Wilson

Books of the Century for the Modern Library

139

50. *Samuel Johnson,* Walter Jackson Bate
51. *The Autobiography of Malcolm X,* Malcolm X and Alex Haley
52. *The Right Stuff,* Tom Wolfe
53. *Eminent Victorians,* Lytton Strachey
54. *Working,* Studs Terkel
55. *Darkness Visible,* William Styron
56. *The Liberal Imagination,* Lionel Trilling
57. *The Second World War,* Winston Churchill
58. *Out of Africa,* Isak Dinesen
59. *Jefferson and His Time,* Dumas Malone
60. *In the American Grain,* William Carlos Williams
61. *Cadillac Desert,* Marc Reisner
62. *The House of Morgan,* Ron Chernow
63. *The Sweet Science,* A. J. Liebling
64. *The Open Society and Its Enemies,* Karl Popper
65. *The Art of Memory,* Frances A. Yates
66. *Religion and the Rise of Capitalism,* R. H. Tawney
67. *A Preface to Morals,* Walter Lippman
68. *The Gate of Heavenly Peace,* Jonathan D. Spence
69. *The Structure of Scientific Revolutions,* Thomas S. Kuhn
70. *The Strange Career of Jim Crow,* C. Vann Woodward
71. *The Rise of the West,* William H. McNeill
72. *The Gnostic Gospels,* Elaine Pagels
73. *James Joyce,* Richard Ellmann
74. *Florence Nightingale,* Cecil Woodham-Smith
75. *The Great War and Modern Memory,* Paul Fussell
76. *The City in History,* Lewis Mumford
77. *Battle Cry of Freedom,* James M. McPherson
78. *Why We Can't Wait,* Martin Luther King Jr.
79. *The Rise of Theodore Roosevelt,* Edmund Morris
80. *Studies in Iconology,* Erwin Panofsky
81. *The Face of Battle,* John Keegan
82. *The Strange Death of Liberal England,* George Dangerfield

83. *Vermeer,* Lawrence Gowing
84. *A Bright Shining Lie,* Neil Sheehan
85. *West with the Night,* Beryl Markham
86. *This Boy's Life,* Tobias Wolff
87. *A Mathematician's Apology,* G. H. Hardy

88. *Six Easy Pieces,* Richard P. Feynman
89. *Pilgrim at Tinker Creek,* Annie Dillard
90. *The Golden Bough,* James George Frazer
91. *Shadow and Act,* Ralph Ellison

Fiction

The Modern Library also made its choices of the one hundred best works of fiction from the twentieth century. Once again, few if any could be labeled religious fiction, but many show indications of religious influence. While Christians should selectively read these volumes, there are rewards in seeing how human nature, in both its degradation and redemption, reflects the reality of God's revelation through his Word.

Books of the Century for the Modern Library

18. *Slaughterhouse-Five*, Kurt Vonnegut
19. *Invisible Man*, Ralph Ellison
20. *Native Son*, Richard Wright
21. *Henderson the Rain King*, Saul Bellow
22. *Appointment to Samarra*, John O'Hara
23. *U.S.A.* (trilogy), John Dos Passos
24. *Winesburg, Ohio*, Sherwood Anderson
25. *A Passage to India*, E. M. Forster
26. *The Wings of the Dove*, Henry James
27. *The Ambassadors*, Henry James
28. *Tender Is the Night*, F. Scott Fitzgerald
29. *Studs Lonigan: A Trilogy*, James T. Farrell
30. *The Good Soldier*, Ford Madox Ford
31. *Animal Farm*, George Orwell
32. *The Golden Bowl*, Henry James
33. *Sister Carrie*, Theodore Dreiser
34. *A Handful of Dust*, Evelyn Waugh
35. *As I Lay Dying*, William Faulkner
36. *All the King's Men*, Robert Penn Warren
37. *The Bridge of San Luis Rey*, Thornton Wilder
38. *Howards End*, E. M. Forster
39. *Go Tell It on the Mountain*, James Baldwin
40. *The Heart of the Matter*, Graham Greene
41. *Lord of the Flies*, William Golding
42. *Deliverance*, James Dickey
43. *A Dance to the Music of Time* (series), Anthony Powell
44. *Point Counter Point*, Aldous Huxley
45. *The Sun Also Rises*, Ernest Hemingway
46. *The Secret Agent*, Joseph Conrad
47. *Nostromo*, Joseph Conrad
48. *The Rainbow*, D. H. Lawrence
49. *Women in Love*, D. H. Lawrence
50. *Tropic of Cancer*, Henry Miller

51. *The Naked and the Dead*, Norman Mailer
52. *Portnoy's Complaint*, Philip Roth
53. *Pale Fire*, Vladimir Nabokov
54. *Light in August*, William Faulkner
55. *On the Road*, Jack Kerouac

56. *The Maltese Falcon*, Dashiell Hammett
57. *Parade's End*, Ford Madox Ford
58. *The Age of Innocence*, Edith Wharton
59. *Zuleika Dobson*, Max Beerbohm

60. *The Moviegoer*, Walker Percy
61. *Death Comes for the Archbishop*, Willa Cather
62. *From Here to Eternity*, James Jones
63. *The Wapshot Chronicle*, John Cheever
64. *The Catcher in the Rye*, J. D. Salinger
65. *A Clockwork Orange*, Anthony Burgess
66. *Of Human Bondage*, W. Somerset Maugham
67. *Heart of Darkness*, Joseph Conrad
68. *Main Street*, Sinclair Lewis
69. *The House of Mirth*, Edith Wharton
70. *The Alexandria Quartet*, Lawrence Durrell
71. *A High Wind in Jamaica*, Richard Hughes
72. *A House for Mr. Biswas*, V. S. Naipaul
73. *The Day of the Locust*, Nathanial West
74. *A Farewell to Arms*, Ernest Hemingway
75. *Scoop*, Evelyn Waugh
76. *The Prime of Miss Jean Brodie*, Muriel Spark
77. *Finnegans Wake*, James Joyce
78. *Kim*, Rudyard Kipling
79. *A Room with a View*, E. M. Forster
80. *Brideshead Revisited*, Evelyn Waugh
81. *The Adventures of Augie March*, Saul Bellow
82. *Angle of Repose*, Wallace Stegner
83. *A Bend in the River*, V. S. Naipaul
84. *The Death of the Heart*, Elizabeth Bowen
85. *Lord Jim*, Joseph Conrad
86. *Ragtime*, E. L. Doctorow
87. *The Old Wives' Tale*, Arnold Bennett
88. *The Call of the Wild*, Jack London
89. *Loving*, Henry Green
90. *Midnight's Children*, Salman Rushdie
91. *Tobacco Road*, Erskine Caldwell
92. *Ironweed*, William Kennedy
93. *The Magus*, John Fowles
94. *Wide Sargasso Sea*, Jean Rhys
95. *Under the Net*, Iris Murdoch
96. *Sophie's Choice*, William Styron
97. *The Sheltering Sky*, Paul Bowles
98. *The Postman Always Rings Twice*, James M. Cain
99. *The Ginger Man*, J. P. Donleavy
100. *The Magnificent Ambersons*, Booth Tarkington

❖

David McKenna served for thirty-three consecutive years as a college, university, and seminary president in Christian higher education. At Spring Arbor College, he developed a junior college into a four-year Christian liberal arts college; at Seattle Pacific University, he led the transition for a four-year college to university status; and at Asbury Theological Seminary, he guided the largest grant ever given in American history to a free-standing graduate school of theology. In 1994, he retired from the presidency to write, consult, and serve as chairman of the board of trustees at Spring Arbor College. McKenna is the author of twenty-one books that range across the fields of psychology, biblical commentary, leadership, history, and theology. An avid reader as well as writer, *How to Read a Christian Book* brings into focus his interest in assisting the laity to be discerning readers of Christian books that advance understanding of the faith and nurture spiritual growth.

In 2000, David and his wife, Janet, celebrated their fiftieth wedding anniversary. Four children and ten grandchildren bring them continuing joy.